Inspiring | Educating | Creating | Entertaining

Brimming with creative inspiration, how-to projects, and useful information to enrich your everyday life, Quarto Knows is a favorite destination for those pursuing their interests and passions. Visit our site and dig deeper with our books into your area of interest: Quarto Creates, Quarto Cooks, Quarto Homes, Quarto Lives, Quarto Drives, Quarto Explores, Quarto Gifts, or Quarto Kids.

First Published in 2020 by Cool Springs Press, an imprint of The Quarto Group, 100 Cummings Center, Suite 265-D, Beverly, MA 01915, USA.
T (978) 282-9590 F (978) 283-2742 QuartoKnows.com

Cool Springs Press titles are also available at discount for retail, wholesale, promotional, and bulk purchase. For details, contact the Special Sales Manager by email at specialsales@quarto.com or by mail at The Quarto Group, Attn: Special Sales Manager, 100 Cummings Center, Suite 265-D, Beverly, MA 01915, USA.

24 23 22 21 20   1 2 3 4 5

ISBN: 978-0-7603-6627-1

Digital edition published in 2020
eISBN: 978-0-7603-6628-8

Library of Congress Cataloging-in-Publication Data
Names: Mattus, Matt, 1959- author.
Title: Mastering the art of flower gardening: a gardener's guide to
  growing flowers, from today's favorites to unusual varieties / Matt
  Mattus.
Description: Beverly, MA : Cool Springs Press, 2020. | Includes index. |
  Summary: "Mastering the Art of Flower Gardening is a lushly illustrated
  book with highly practical, firsthand tips on how to grow truly
  interesting and unusual flowers"-- Provided by publisher.
Identifiers: LCCN 2019050169 (print) | LCCN 2019050170 (ebook) | ISBN
  9780760366271 | ISBN 9780760366288 (ebook)
Subjects: LCSH: Flower gardening.
Classification: LCC SB405 .M412 2020 (print) | LCC SB405 (ebook) | DDC
  635.9--dc23
LC record available at https://lccn.loc.gov/2019050169
LC ebook record available at https://lccn.loc.gov/2019050170

Design: Megan Jones Design
Cover Images: Matt Mattus
Page Layout: Megan Jones Design
Photography: Matt Muttus, except by Shutterstock on pages 29 (right), 45 (top), 48, 55, 72, 79, 83, 86, 102 (right), 103 (left), 133, 147, 154, 159, and otherwise noted.

Printed in China

MASTERING
the ART *of*
FLOWER
GARDENING

**A GARDENER'S GUIDE TO GROWING FLOWERS,
FROM TODAY'S FAVORITES TO UNUSUAL VARIETIES**

MATT MATTUS

COOL
SPRINGS
PRESS

CONTENTS

◀ Cafe au Lait Dahlia

INTRODUCTION

Of all the plants we might choose to grow, flowers may be considered to be the most trivial. Even my older brother, Bruce, who is a rather capable gardener himself, teases me about it. After he found out that I wrote a book on vegetable gardening, he said, "I thought all you grew in that greenhouse were flowers?" Whenever I offer to drive a few flats of Spencer sweet peas over to his house, he asks me if they are the edible ones or "those flowers you grow."

It always drove me crazy when friends at work would ask how my flowers were doing, assuming that anyone who gardens just raises flowers. The answer is that while of course I grow flowers (and plenty of them), I have never described my passion with plants as "flower growing."

People who know me are aware that I am first and foremost a plant collector, a horticulturist, a "plantsman" (a 10th-century term for one who is serious about all types of plants, not just flowers). Still, I often feel the need to protest my "flower-growing" moniker, as it sounds trivial or not serious enough. Plants in my collection may bloom but blooms alone aren't why I grow them. I cultivate them because these plants provide pleasure, either because of how rare they are, how they work with a collection, or how challenging they are to grow. It's more common today for houseplants and flowers to be treated more as decor than botanically interesting specimens. Flowers can be tremendously meaningful. They can brighten a room or convey emotions in ways words sometimes can't—and provide beauty. We grow them in our gardens and pick them to arrange in our homes to provide joy for ourselves, friends, and family. They are also pretty fun to grow.

I consider myself obsessed with flowers for many reasons: their use in history, their use in the arts, why people grow them, the fascination certain eras and cultures had with them, how they fell out of fashion and came back into fashion, and how they have been commoditized. As an artist, I look at how plants and their flowers are used in landscape, floral, and garden design.

I am well aware that while most of these uses are based on long-established principals, they also are fluid enough for flexibility and personal expression.

In these pages, I may not shy away from expressing some basic rules (proven ones like seeds that grow best if direct-sown. However, as any horticulturist knows, many of these rules can be broken—but never casually. You should know why a seed grows better if direct-sown but also how to effectively work your way through the "cheat" of growing it in a pot. I share many of those tips in this book.

Much of the fun in gardening is curating a spectacular bed or collection. Since we all can choose what we want to grow, my greatest wish is that this book will inspire you to reach higher. To learn not to buy everything on one nursery visit or from a single seed catalog. Just as the Internet has opened up a broader palette for your kitchen, it also opens up the entire world of seeds and plants for your garden.

Within these pages, I touch on many of the lost 19th-century horticultural crafts gardeners practiced, such as forcing lily of the valley pips into bloom or raising tuberoses and mignonette in the home garden. Some flowers haven't been seen or experienced by most of us for over a century, like the fragrant parma violets that were once more popular than most any cut flower in a Valentine's Day or winter bouquet. The modern horticultural systems that bring us micro-propagated plants cloned by the millions worldwide, which I celebrate and support, comes with a cost—the loss of many of the most precious rare flowers hardly grown today. My hope is that just as recent food movements have brought about artisanal products and local specialties, flowers and plants will soon follow. It's not an enormous leap, as 150 years ago, all flowers and seedlings were grown locally. The trend may already be starting with the advent of Deborah Prinzing's Slow Flower movement and rise of local flower farms.

Above: Scabiosa 'Oxford Blue'

Much about horticulture has advanced over the 20th century to today. Far better plants are being bred and introduced. Larger retail nurseries have become bigger, while small mom-and-pop nurseries have closed. The entire business of horticulture has been streamlined and feels more like traditional product design than anything else. It needed to—like any product, a plant needs to sit on a shelf or fit on a truck and ultimately sell at retail, or it won't be grown.

While this makes good business sense for big-box stores, it comes at a cost to us. My hope is that with trends being driven by local flower growers, small independent nurseries will begin to adapt and try not to fit into the larger horticultural model of commercial seeds and patented plugs, which seems inefficient when the store down the road offers the same products at a lower cost. My hope is that the independent growers will educate themselves and start growing plants and flowers of more interesting varieties. Artisanal selections of horticulturally interesting flowers are not all that different than local cheeses, local brewed beer, or handmade sausages. It will just take time

to educate home growers that both big-box retail brands and interesting curiosities or heirloom flowers can live harmoniously in their gardens.

In this book, I cover both common and unusual flowers. Think of it as gaining access to the wish list of a horticulturist at a leading botanic garden. These are some of the finest old-fashioned annuals, biennials, and perennials you can get today, and most are not anything you will find at a garden center. A good number of the annual flowers in this book might even be new to you. Many are true antiques, and while they can be hard to find even as seed, I offer sources in the back that will help you.

Some of these plant names do not roll easily off the tongue (even I confuse phacelia and felicia, or vaccaria and viscaria). You may never see old-fashioned plants like salpiglossis and schizanthus at a big-box store or large garden center, but they are growable at home by most gardeners. If you want annual poppies, sweet peas, or even the best cut flower, like larkspurs, there really are few options other than starting them at home. Only a few nurseries know at what stage to properly offer them (when they're still tiny and not yet budding).

The rest of the book is dedicated to long-time favorites and how to grow them. We all might know how to grow a dahlia or think that a wisteria is a weedy vine, but do we all know how to dig and save dahlia bulbs properly or how to train a wisteria into a tree form? I also touch of some horticultural craft that may be interesting for more advanced gardeners, such as Japanese trained chrysanthemums, fragrant tuberoses, or how to force unusual indoor bulbs. There is something for every level of gardener here, growing South African *Lachenalia* bulbs to getting a good crop of paperwhites going for the holidays. Regardless of how much of a green thumb you have, I encourage you to at least try some of the more challenging species just once (or twice, as most of us do). Gardening is about growing and learning, but it's also about having fun and experiencing joy in both failure and success.

—MATT

Opposite: Trumpet lilies and fragrant intersectional lilies are the official favorite flower in our garden. Armloads come into the house, and while they have nearly too strong of a fragrance, we tolerate it for a few weeks in July. Above: Tree peony 'Shimane Cho Juraka'

GETTING STARTED

There are as many ways to sow seeds as there are people writing about it. In this section, I will share commonly recommended ways as well as some secrets I know and have had success with. Many of the flowers in this book come with the advice that they must be direct-sown, but here's a secret few garden writers ever mention—most of these seeds can be started in individual modules, though the task can be tricky. Still, it's the way most estate gardeners and horticulturalists at large botanic gardens grow their annual poppies and hard-to-transplant flowers. It can be done but only if you have the right environment (a greenhouse or bright garage window) with perfect *temperature* control. It's not a task for the casual gardeners, but I feel that you need to be in on the secret. It can be done. Believe me, only the most romantic of private-estate gardeners or the most inexperienced botanic garden horticulturists actually take the time to "sprinkle annual poppy seed on top of the snow" willy-nilly in late winter. I know I don't.

PLANTS OR SEEDS

I am not ashamed to say that I "cheat" and take the easier route of buying many of my annuals from the handful of small nurseries that are able to grow many of the hard-to-find and challenging-to-start cool-weather annuals. I do have a greenhouse, however, so I start some of these myself, as I am always up for a challenge. I try to improve my sowing skills every year, especially with annuals that I either cannot find at local nurseries or that are mistreated if grown commercially, such as snapdragons or asters.

I have nothing against big garden centers and nurseries, and in fact I fully support their efforts and products. I can't imagine any other time in the history of gardening when there have been so many new amazing varieties for us to grow. I especially support branded varieties (such as Proven Winners), as many of these are the latest and greatest introductions coming from independent plant breeders. Most are indeed over-performers and are either sterile (meaning they don't produce seed) so they bloom all summer endlessly, or just superior varieties. They do cost more, but more often than not, they are worth the price.

I don't have time to fuss with most plants, and especially considering the number of flowers that I grow, I like do-gooders. I balance what I buy and what I choose to grow similarly to how I grow vegetables. If I can buy fresh zucchini at my local farmers market all summer long, why do I need to grow it in my garden? Because garden real estate is precious, I would be better off growing something that I cannot find anywhere. I do the same with choosing what flowers to grow from seed.

I buy many seed-raised annuals at commercial nurseries and garden centers, but I also buy plenty from a few local specialty growers who grow very special annuals. These growers are not in every community, but they are becoming more popular with the rise of local farming, CSAs, and flower farmers. Some flower farmers even sell their plugs to gardeners if they are able to buy an entire flat of plugs, and some local independent backyard growers are offering unusual annuals raised from seed. You may have to drive a couple of hours, but it's worth it if you want a pack of perfectly grown larkspurs or salpiglossis at the right stage for planting out.

Most big garden centers work within a completely different development cycle and timeline. They are about production and about moving product. They excel at moving branded named varieties because they order them from plug growers and liner growers months ahead of time. These growers need to know in advance what seed or cuttings to get, and since many of the best annuals are patented, the system often requires licensing fees up front

Individually sown Papaver somniferum 'Lauren's Grape' plants ready for transplanting.

These Primula veris (Oxlips) are among the easiest primroses to raise from seed.

to ensure that royalties are paid to everyone involved, from the backyard plant breeder who created the plant to the propagator, agent, or plug grower down the line.

I fully support patented plants, as they ensure that the time and efforts of the plant breeders are addressed. I know plenty of them, and before plant patents, they could not support their families. It's a good thing to support, and even though you may feel that everything has "gone corporate," the truth is that many now benefit from the research and development, as the royalties are often shared across all levels of product development. This product development it not only involves plant breeding and science but also marketing, buying, branding, and packaging. The annuals that make it through this system are far superior to most older strains (particularly calibrachoa or nemesia).

I also support independent growers and those who raise hard-to-grow annuals for those who appreciate them. Most every region has that special backyard grower or small nursery that specializes in seed-raised annuals or propagates special plants that every horticulturist wants. If you're unsure where these nurseries are, try asking a horticulturist at your local botanic garden for some names, or join a local plant society. These sources are rarely secret—they are just invisible to most casual gardeners.

I live in Massachusetts, but I drive an hour and a half to Vermont where two such sources happen to be in the same town. I know that I can buy flats of perfectly grown, hard-to-find annuals at Walker's Farm Stand in Dummerston, and just a couple of miles away, I can find even rarer annuals at the Bunker Farm, a seasonal family farm run by Helen O'Donnell and her family. Most of the flowers in this book can be bought at the Bunker Farm (no mail order). In California, Annie's Annuals (which does ship seasonally) carries many as well.

TOOLS

As most seeds are tiny and difficult to handle, a syringe-style precision vacuum seeder works very well. Larger seeds must still be sown individually, but the task is easier with handheld seeders like a small plastic seed dispenser that allows you to tap gently and adjust the setting to allow one or two seeds to drop into each cell or plug.

If sowing directly in the garden, the best trick, especially useful with poppy seed, is to mix the seed with sand and use a kitchen sieve to dust the seed medium lightly over the ground. The goal is to get some distance between seedlings, as transplanting seedlings that have germinated is much harder to do successfully. In cells or containers, even difficult-to-transplant seedlings will produce a few roots that are not touching the sides of the pot, so they are less damaged if transplanted gently.

RAISING FLOWERS FROM SEED

Finding a local source for many of the flowers in this book is a great option, but if you are unable to find one, everything here is growable by you at your home. While most gardening books will offer two basic methods for sowing seeds (direct-sowing outdoors or starting early inside or under glass), the rules are fuzzier than that, especially if you speak to anyone who has been gardening for a long time.

When it comes to seed sowing, there are some very strict guidelines to follow. Usually those rules involve covering the seed, the amount of light needed to germinate, or anything to do with the optimal temperatures for germination. These are things you want to pay attention to, yet because most rules are made to be broken, there plenty of ways to start seeds. Many of the ways offered in gardening

Left: Having the proper tools and materials will make all the difference in the world when it comes to seed starting—whether you start early under LED lights, in your cellar or garage, or in a greenhouse. Many sites sell professional cell or plug trays essential for plants that resent root disturbance, as well as soil-block makers, handheld seeding aids like vacuum dispensors as well as mini-greenhouses and heating mats. Top, right: Handheld seed dispensers are inexpensive yet indispensable in spacing seeds properly in cell trays or modules, especially where one or two small seeds must be set into each cell. Most are adjustable. Bottom, right: For very tiny seeds, a hand-held vacuum device is often the only tool for the job. Most come with syringe tips that with a bit of practice, will allow you to sow even the tiniest seeds one-by-one such as poppies or primula.

books or on blogs can even contradict each other, but for some of us, the seeds will still grow. They are seeds, and biologically they are designed to grow.

I imagine that many of you sometimes just tear open packets of seeds and sow them in rows in a flat and set them under lights. I grew up watching my parents do that, and generally most of the seeds grew and flowered. Yet every seed and every plant has an ideal sowing method, and it is good to first know what that ideal is and then adjust from there given your conditions.

Let's take direct-sown flowers, for example, for those are some of the more challenging flowers to grow, particularly if they have tiny seeds. While it is true that a direct-sown poppy will out-perform even the most carefully coddled seedling from a plug tray, most of us will have the best luck somewhere in between. I never read advice in books about how to start poppies in containers, yet I know of many small nurseries and botanic gardens who do this very well (as do I). While it isn't ideal nor easy, it often is

the best way to get seedlings off to a good start for gardeners with a shorter cool growing season, and it is how most flower farmers and estate gardeners start their flowers. The same goes for larkspurs and many of the "never ever transplant" annuals. Just pay attention to each of their needs and transplant them accordingly.

Though the rules can be bent for home-grown seeds, avoid buying certain annuals at garden centers if they have been grown improperly. Zinnias and cosmos will sulk and stay short if they are purchased too old in a six-pack. Most garden centers sell annuals in bloom or they won't make it out the door. This is okay for some annuals such as pansies, violas, nemesia, and calibrachoa. But others such as cosmos or snapdragons, and certainly any of the hard-to-transplant annuals such as salpiglossis, poppies, larkspurs, and most of the cool-growing annuals, must never be in bloom. They must be transplanted when they are very young, with two sets of leaves at the most.

METHODS FOR STARTING SEEDS OUTDOORS

METHOD 1: FOLLOWING THE RULES

Direct-sowing the conventional way means sowing the seed of the plant you are growing outdoors, right where the plants will be growing. Most plants that need to be direct-sown resent any root disturbance. Generally they have special roots designed for certain soil and environmental conditions. Examples include taproots, which form early and must never touch the bottom of a pot (like carrots), or hair-like fibrous roots that are too delicate to handle their growing medium being disturbed in anyway.

- Sow seeds in late winter or early spring directly onto the surface of the soil as soon as it is drained and can be raked. Often light freezes and frosts won't hurt hard the seeds, as the seedlings will thus emerge at the proper time.

- Be conscious about the site of the seedbed, as transplanting elsewhere is not recommended.

- Sprinkle seed (mixed with grit or fine sand if the seeds are small to distribute them evenly) onto the surface of the raked soil.

- Carefully thin seedlings as soon as they emerge (rather than pricking them out), and allow space for the mature plants to grow.

- For optimum results, resist the urge to transplant seedlings. Keep an eye on weeds and watering as well as foot traffic from pets and children, especially when the seedlings are young, as most will be very small.

TOP: Sprinkle seed into dry sand to help distribute it evenly.
TOP RIGHT: Sift seed over prepared (raked) ground and water.
MIDDLE: Protect for the first few weeks with poultry wire so that tiny seedlings won't get trampled by little feet or paws.
BOTTOM: Provide stakes or small twigs to support tender stems of annuals like poppies.

METHOD 2: BREAKING THE RULES

Some direct-sown seeds can be started in individual cells or pots set outdoors where it's cold and bright (a cold frame, unheated garage window, on a deck). Though unconventional, this method works well for many cool-weather annuals—those which typically only come with the strict advice to 'sow where they are to grow'. Try it with larkspurs (pictured here) or annual poppies.

SAVE INDOOR SEED SOWING
FOR RARER OR SLOWER-GROWING ANNUALS

Save valuable space under lighting units for those harder-to-find annuals that must be started 8–10 weeks early in warmth which share space with my tomatoes and eggplants under LED lights. They get planted outdoors around the same time after the soil has fully warmed up and all threats of frost have passed. Flowers like the African Foxglove or *Ceratotheca* (at right) get this treatment, as do other heat-lovers like *Tithonia* (at far right).

METHODS FOR STARTING SEEDS INDOORS

While the best results come from seeds sown on site since light and temperature shifts naturally help keep these seedlings sturdy, if you are conscientious and clever, some seeds can be started indoors.

Direct-sown seeds prefer a cold or cool start, with bright light and buoyant breezes. While a greenhouse or a sunny glassed-in porch may be best, artificial LED lights (because they are cooler) in a cellar or a garage may suffice. Materials for seed starting are a bit more, but the entire process is becoming easier with the use of newly available cell or extra-deep plug trays (5 or 6 inches [13 to 15 cm] deep), which allows roots to grow deep.

METHOD 1: WARM WEATHER ANNUALS

Some plants in this book are warm-weather annuals, which benefit from being sown indoors due to their love of warm weather at all stages of their growth. Amaranthus, emilia, Malva, Malope and Resela all resent root disturbance but benefit from an early warm start, so they can be sown early if one can get excellent light quality. LEDs and fluorescent tubes rarely do this as effectively as sunlight though, so on the brightest spring days, it's good to move flats outdoors to get full sunlight and the benefits of wind, which will strengthen their stems.

METHOD 2: COOL WEATHER ANNUALS

These more resilient annuals can tolerate some root disturbance if handled gently, but generally, they require an early start indoors because they are slower growing and thus benefit from an extended growing season. For most northern gardeners, they are impractical to sow directly outdoors. The list includes snapdragons, larkspurs, and others. Cooler growing conditions are usually best after germination, but always check specific cultural requirements listed for each species. Transplanting up into gradually larger containers is often beneficial, as is the typical hardening-off before planting outdoors, even if a species is considered cold tolerant. Always check the specific requirements for temperature and cultural needs for each variety.

Young Malope seedlings sown indoors under lights to take advantage of the warmth, are moved out to the greenhouse by April to take advantage of the bright spring sunshine.

The trick to getting many warm-weather annuals off to an early start is heat and bright light. These Mignonette (Reseda odorata) seedlings started under lights in our cellar and transplanted to larger pots in April when they can handle cooler temperatures in the greenhouse.

- Sow these slow growers 8 to 10 weeks early indoors.

- Transplant into individual cells or pots at the second-leaf stage.

- Follow guidelines for unique cultural requirements such as temperature.

TECHNIQUE FOR SEEDS TO SOW INDOORS OR OUTDOORS

These are annuals can be started indoors 4 to 6 weeks before planting out to get a jump on the season. This group includes some of the easiest to grow annuals, such as zinnia, marigolds, and asters. Know that this process helps you more than it helps them, for these seeds will grow into far healthier plants if you wait and sow them outdoors once the soil has warmed enough that you can plant tomatoes. A zinnia is often thought of as an easy-to-transplant seedling, but the truth is that it resents transplanting, and any direct-sown zinnias will outperform prestarted six-pack zinnias in just a few weeks. Sprinkle a row of zinnia seeds into your garden next July and let me know how they did compared to those apparently healthy, thick green-stemmed starts you bought at a garden center in May. You'll be shocked.

- Cosmos, calendula, zinnia, and marigold: Quick to germinate, these will tolerate moderate root disturbance and can be sown closer together in seed flats into rows, and then transplanted into cell packs by the second leaf stage.

- Sunflower, nasturtium, safflower, cerinthe: While easy and quick to germinate, these will suffer a bit if roots are disturbed and benefit from careful spacing. You can also sow into individual pots and then carefully slip them into the garden.

SPRING BLOOMS

Spring is the natural season of rebirth, seed-starting, and hope. Gardeners know it is a time of great excitement but also of transitional weather that is unpredictable, regardless of where you live and garden.

Gardening is so intimately connected to nature, but sometimes we forget that while a natural process, it often involves plant species from other parts of the world. Most gardeners are integrating populations of plants and flowers from distant places. For example, tulips may have been breed and cultivated in the Netherlands, but their wild relatives came from Turkey or Kazakhstan. Some cool-weather annuals might be native to the Pacific coast in North America. Starting them from seed requires adjustment to our particular climates, so spring flowers for some might be winter flowers for others.

Essentially, it's important to know as a flower gardener that seasons are relative. For most of us, it's often "meteorological spring" that seems to make more sense than astronomical or calendrical spring. In the northern climates, gardeners center their growing lives around that mystical frost-free date that never seems to arrive as a set date on the calendar but rather as a day that somehow passes a few weeks earlier before we know it. Regardless of season or climate, we usually know it's safe to plant tender plants outdoors once native trees have produced their first tiny leaves.

It really doesn't matter if you experience spring in the Northern Hemisphere (March through May) or Southern Hemisphere (September through December). Spring and flowers are synonymous everywhere. Spring marks the start of the primary gardening season and the start of the floral extravaganza we all strive for.

◄ Instead of using a single color when bedding out tulips in a display border, try mixing multiple varieties, curating your own color mix.

ABOVE: The tiered branching of *Cornus controversa* 'Variegeta' puts on a show nearly as nice as any flower can in our spring garden.

RIGHT: Be sure to celebrate spring by planting enough bulbs in out-of-the-way places like the vegetable garden so that you can pick bunches to bring indoors.

LEFT: *Primula veris,* the 'Cowslip' is another easy primose to raise from seed.

ABOVE: Standard Dwarf Bearded Iris

ABOVE: The species or horticultural crocus are some of the easiest bulbs to force after their prerequisite 12-week chilling where pots won't freeze, but are kept below 40°F. If potted in early October, pots like these chrysanthemums bloom in just a matter of weeks if coaxed with gradually warming temperatures on a cold windowsill or greenhouse.

RIGHT: Lunaria annua is commonly known as 'Honesty' or 'The Silver-Dollar plant' (because of its dried, coin-like seed pods in fall). While it can be an aggressive self-seeder few of us ever consider it as an attractive quick-growing flower for the border.

SNOWDROP
Galanthus spp.

CROCUS
Crocus spp.

If snowdrops bloomed in mid-summer we might overlook them, but as the first harbinger of spring, they're addition to our gardens is invaluable. Some snowdrops in my garden date back to the 1950s. Snowdrop collectors are obsessed with the nearly 500 named cultivars and 20 or so species. They do all look kind of the same, however. The easiest specimens to recognize are the double-flowered ones like 'Flore Pleno' or the rarer 'Blewbury Tart'. Most common will be *Galanthus nivalis* named selections, a double flowered form or two, and the *G. elwesii*, the giant snowdrop, which is about 25 percent larger and not as quick to spread, so it should be planted in larger colonies.

- Order snowdrops in late summer.
- Unlike other hardy bulbs, *Galanthus* dislike being dug up and dried off. Buy and plant them immediately.
- Naturally woodland plants, snowdrops look best in wild or natural-looking gardens.
- *Galanthus* enjoy companion plants and ground covers. English ivy (*Hedera* spp.), all ferns, and *Vinca* make good companion plants.

The genus *Crocus* is just about the easiest of all spring flowering bulbs to grow with the least effort. Crocus is a large genus with over 90 species, but only a handful are commonly available from bulb catalogs. Crocuses add joy to a garden, and they bloom with little effort just as the snow is melting. Though most associate crocus with early spring, don't overlook the fall blooming species, of which there are many. The main types of spring crocuses are *C. vernus* (*C. × cultorum*), which come in many shades of purple, white, lavender, and striped. They are always the showiest in the garden.

- Crocuses are easy to grow and will divide to form congested clumps if allowed to go dry during the summer heat (turn off irrigation).
- Plant crocus corms in clusters and in great numbers if possible.
- All crocuses are easy to force into bloom indoors.

HELLEBORE

Helleborus spp.

WINTER ACONITE

Eranthis hyemalis

You can't have too many hellebores in your garden. These lovely winter or early-spring blooming plants do need some special attention upfront, however, they are slow to establish and should be planted into the garden after blooming in spring so that they can live undisturbed for years. Like peonies, hellebores should be treated as an investment or heritage plant.

- Plants in the north need to be well rooted in rich woodland soil augmented with ground limestone.

- If planting a mature plant in a pot, do not jumble the rootball or you may sacrifice next year's flowers.

- Success with hellebores will come from choosing the best variety and planting the smallest plant you can find.

- Resist cutting or removing damaged foliage in late winter until flower buds emerge.

- With dozens of named varieties and interspecific crosses, always check the hardiness zone suggested for your climate.

- A plant native to open, deciduous woodlands, hellebores thrive best under trees with deep root systems and with light shade in the summer months.

Success with the winter aconite can seem futile. The trick is simple though, for these relatives of the buttercup family share something with snowdrops: they dislike being dug up and shipped. As such, the easiest foolproof way of getting winter aconites in your garden is to find someone else who has had luck with them and transplant some in spring into your own garden. Happy in partially shaded lawn plantings or in an open woodland, they will multiply.

- Order bulbs from a reputable Dutch bulb dealer online (order early).

- Ask a friend if they'll share transplants or seedlings from their garden or woodland where they have may naturalized. Dig just after they have bloomed and while still in growth.

- Plant immediately upon arrival in an area of your garden where they are unlikely to be disturbed for many years.

NARCISSUS

Narcissus spp.

Also known as daffodils or jonquils, narcissus are one of the most commonly grown bulbs on the planet. They bloom in early spring just when we really need some color. Many are fragrant, all are cheerful, and most are long-lived. Narcissus can be fancy and showy or tiny and demure. There are giant, blousy bright-colored hybrids, graceful tiny miniatures, and wild species that are highly collectable and treasured.

- Narcissus are classified in distinct groups based upon flower form, size, and sometimes color. These divisions are good to learn even if you are a beginner. They help you understand the various groups and sizes of daffodils, which includes thousands of named hybrids.

- Plant pointed end up in soil that has a bit of slow-release organic fertilizer.

- Water is essential in spring and while they are growing but should be reduced once the plants bloom.

- Deer restant and long-lived if one allows the foliage to mature and fade undisturbed in early summer.

TULIP

Tulipa spp.

The tulip is making a comeback thanks to flower farmers and flower lovers who are beginning to appreciate this most famous of spring bulb flowers. Like many bulbs, choosing a tulip variety comes down to personal preference (I have my favorites, like any striped tulip, heirloom varieties, or the magical orange and violet 'Prinses Irene', but really—is there a bad tulip?) Species types are less showy but often longer lived in the garden. Any tricks with tulips often come down to how they were stored while they were dormant.

- More than most bulbs, tulips are sensitive to storage temperatures, which can dry out the embryonic flower bud deep inside each bulb.

- Tulips must be planted not too early and not too late. The ideal Goldilocks temperature for the soil is below 60°F (16°C).

- Animals will eat tulip bulbs (but never narcissus), so cover beds with chicken wire or construct bulb boxes to discourage squirrels.

- Tulips look best if the plants are close together, nearly touching, and in great numbers.

HYACINTH
Hyacinthus orientalis

WOODLAND ANEMONES
Anemone spp.

AT-A-GLANCE

No scent says spring like hyacinth. While I grow most of my hyacinths in pots to force for indoor winter displays, a few are saved for the garden, where I often prefer the looser-flowering varieties. Once sold as Roman hyacinths, they are now an improved strain known as multifestival hyacinths and can produce up to six stalks per bulb. However, a fancy Dutch hybrid will eventually grow weaker in the years after planting, producing a more natural, less dense floral display.

- Hyacinths look best if planted close together, either in formal rows or in large clumps.

- Hyacinths are deer-proof and good pollinator plants for bees.

- They like well-draining soil.

- Hyacinth bulbs can cause a rash, so wear gloves when handling them.

- In early spring, garden centers are beginning to offer bulbs prechilled and sprouting, which are worth adding to containers or to the garden for those who may have forgotten to plant any the previous autumn.

The ephemeral anemones, like many named cultivars of *Anemone nemorosa*, as well as *A. ranunculoides*, and *A. × lipsiensis* and the closely related *Anemonella thalictroides*, are some of the choicest relatives of the large ranunculus family known commonly as anemones. Nothing like the cutflower *A. coronaria* (see page 36), these are small, highly cherished woodland plants that spread slowly and live long. Stay clear, however, of the garden thug, *A. canadensis*. While lovely, it can take over an entire garden. These smaller gems are from the other side of the tracks, and often their price reflects that refinement.

- Plant anemones in gardens with woodland conditions where the plants will not be disturbed.

- Hostas and epimedium are good companions for anemones as they bloom early then disappear for the summer.

- You'll most likely need to order them grown in pots, yet shipped dormant. Look for them in specialty catalogs always ordering in winter for early spring shipment before they sell out.

BLEEDING HEART
Dicentra spectabilis

Beloved by many, the pink or white heart-shaped flowers of this pass-along garden perennial is the classic cottage garden flower. A relative of the poppy family, it can live for decades in gardens of many types with little care. Newer strains feature new colors, from coral to pure white and yellow. Some have lime-tinted foliage. Easy to grow, plants transplant best in spring. They only bloom for a few weeks, but who could live without them?

- Purchase young nursery plants.
- Bleeding heart is partial to light-shade conditions.
- The plants are likely to go dormant by midsummer.
- Bleeding heart grows best in rich loamy soil where it can live undisturbed for years. Best if planted in a spot where you rarely dig or cultivate.

RANUNCULUS
Ranunculus asiaticus

The double-form hybrid *Ranunculus asiaticus* is among the most beautiful of cut flowers. Their fragile-looking, tissue paper-like flowers are grown today in hoop houses by flower farmers much like they were once grown a century or two ago in cold glasshouses. In the north, one finds them sold as forced potted plants for spring displays alongside other cold-tolerant plants like pansy and nemesia. *R. asiaticus* is worth trying only if you have a cold greenhouse or live in a Mediterranean climate like Southern California. Grown from tubers, cutflower varieties can be difficult to find if you are a home grower, but retail nurseries do sell tubers of the more common Tecolote strain.

- Unlike *Anemone coronaria*, the larger ranunculus tubers will grow the nicest flowers.
- Often called "mother bulbs," ranunculus tubers must be soaked in warm water for 6 to 12 hours before planting.
- Outdoors, especially in the north, store-bought plants sold in-bud are easiest way to add ranunculus to the spring garden. Just don't expect them to come back for a second show, as these are strictly tender bulbs.

ALLIUM
Allium spp.

Alliums, or the ornamental onions, are extremely popular today. They are expensive, but few flowers can match their presence in the garden—even for a one-shot show. A massive genus, the onion family has many ornamental alliums that are commonly grown as flowers, but most can be grouped as bulbous onions (the short-lived giants like 'Gladiator' or 'Globemaster' with flowers as big as a softball). Most alliums bloom in spring, but some bloom in summer or in autumn. Most are long-lived and hardy to zone 4, aside from the showy giant types. Always read the catalog descriptions well.

- The large giant alliums, while the showiest, are short-lived in the garden, usually performing for 3 years or less.

- Plant bulbs in the fall, 8 inches (20 cm) deep. In spring, their lush foliage is pretty but is notoriously unsightly, as it naturally fades and turns brown just as they start blooming.

- Some alliums are invasive, so be careful. Most allium sold in the Dutch bulb catalogs are safe, noninvasive, probably sterile, and certainly garden friendly.

ANEMONE CORONARIA
Anemone coronaria

The classic florist cutflower anemones are bright, cheerful, and popular. Anemones and ranunculus provide the backbone of winter and early spring flowers for holidays, weddings, and funerals. Traditionally they have grown well in cold greenhouses when planted in the open ground.

- Vernalization will happen naturally in mild-winter areas where temperatures drop into the mid-20s.
- They grow well as an annual bulb outdoors in zones 8 and up.
- In the north in zones 6 and lower, *Anemone coronaria* rarely does well in open garden and will fail if planted in autumn.
- Smaller tubers will produce more flowers than large ones, which become woody.
- Soak tubers overnight in autumn and store in damp coir in your refrigerator.

FORGET-ME-NOT
Myosotis scorpioides

If you plant forget-me-not once, you will have it forever. A natural self-sower, this near-invasive can take over a garden, but few gardeners hold it against them. Forget-me-nots look best if allowed to form large colonies. If plants become aggressive, any young seedlings that emerge are easy to weed out. A true biennial, the seed can be sown in autumn or early spring for flowering the following year. If your soil remains moist for the summer, any progeny may continue for generations.

- Sow in autumn where spring soil won't be disturbed.

- Choose a partially shaded site with moisture and fertile soil.

- Weed out white-flowered forms as they appear, if you want a completely blue display.

- There are blue, white, and pink selections available at garden centers.

- Forget-Me-Not's can be used effectively in bulb borders, especially when tall tulips are interplanted with them where they grow thickly.

COLUMBINE
Aquilegia spp.

Few flowers are as old-style romantic as columbines. Both the hybrids and heirloom selections pull on our heartstrings, and make us want to add columbine to our gardens. Most hybrids are created from woodland species, so finding the right site where columbine will be happy is half the battle. A short-lived perennial, most columbines behave more like biennials, blooming their best in their second or third year in partially shaded gardens with loamy soil and lots of compost.

- The best plants come from seed, which are easy to grow if the seeds are is fresh or have been prechilled (see Resources, page 233).

- Start seed indoors in late winter and set hardened plants out after frost risks have passed.

- Most seed-raised plants will bloom the following year and will slowly decline but may self-seed.

- Nursery-bought plants won't live long, so resist investing in many.

AT-A-GLANCE

PRIMROSE

Primula spp.

Few flowers conjure romance more than primroses. From English cottage gardens to illustrated nursery rhyme books, primroses charm us and inspire dreams. Yet primroses are an enigma. When was the last time you saw a garden full of primroses? How about a primrose border in full bloom? Have you ever really seen an auricula theater in all of its glory or heard the often-quoted Shakespearian line from Hamlet, "Himself the primrose path of dalliance treads"? Primroses seduce us by name and by their romantic allure, yet they remain largely absent in our gardens.

Botanically, the primrose, or *Primula*, family is massive, with more than 450 species mostly found in the Northern Hemisphere. At least half of them hail from western China and the Himalayas. With so many species, you may wonder why we see so few in gardens today. The answer is not as simple as "primroses are difficult to grow," although they have that reputation. It actually has more to do with the scarcity of primroses at garden centers. Most primrose species just don't fit the basic requirements for commercial nursery trade,

including conformity and speed to market. Plus, the primrose plants you may manage to find today are not always the species best suited for planting in our gardens, they are just more conducive for the needs of the trade and for early spring sales to customers who are desiring some spring color. In fact, most primroses today are hybrids developed specifically for the potted plant industry. They are best used as temporary bedding plants in mild-winter areas such as California, or as even shorter-lived houseplants for cold windowsills in the north.

Nevertheless, primroses are worth adding to your garden; the greatest challenge is to find the right species and cultivars that will live and prosper in your garden. These do take a little bit of effort both to seek out and care for. No special skills are needed to raise them, as most only need a "lift-and-divide" every few years to keep them vigorous. The rewards will far outweigh the labor, especially since these are early spring tasks to be done just when we are yearning to get our hands a little dirty.

◀ This double Auricula primrose was bred and introduced by British primrose breeder Derek Salt in 2002. This treasure isn't the easiest to grow as it prefers cold, dry winter conditions and cool summers, not to mention alkaline soil and excellent drainage. But the results are worth any sacrifice when they are like this.

HOW TO GROW PRIMROSES

If you've attempted to grow primroses and failed, then you know how fussy they can seem. But if you can provide the right conditions, growing them is relatively hands-off for much of the year. In fact, you can grow spectacular primroses if you live in zones 7 and colder. In warmer Southern gardens, unfortunately, you may need to step back from dreaming about primrose paths.

There are no workarounds when it comes to primrose culture—what is required is something you either have or you don't. They are quite particular about climate and habitat, so your success with primroses begins with knowing your garden's conditions and being honest about what species can grow well there. Primroses are one of those plants that are not very adaptable to conditions that don't favor them. For example, I adore all of the candelabra-blooming Asiatic primroses like *P. japonica* or *P. florindae*, but I don't have a stream or a boggy area, so I must accept that I cannot grow them well, or at all. Don't become discouraged though—primroses are quite growable for many gardeners, and many are worth mastering.

Approaching cultivation of *Primula* casually is risky. Making generalizations or assumptions about their needs usually will result in short-lived plants. Do your homework, and don't visit the nursery and simply grab the plant that you think is prettiest. At the same time, do not be intimidated. For the home gardener, there are at least a dozen or so viable primrose varieties that are not hard to find.

Asiatic candelabra primroses *bulleyana*

SOURCING PLANTS AND SEEDS

The greatest challenge with primroses is not caring for them, it is sourcing them. For the most part, the best garden primroses are ones you start from home as seedlings or acquire from someone else who grows them. Gone are the days where a specialty nursery will take you out back and dig one from the field for you. In fact, few nurseries carry more than one or two types of primrose plant, if they carry them at all. No worries though, for primroses can be raised from seed if the seed is guaranteed fresh or has been stratified. You can buy prechilled seed (see Resources, page 233) or join the American Primrose Society and participate in their annual seed exchange, where serious collectors and botanic gardeners turn for their seed.

THE PRIMROSE STORY

Raising primroses was once an artisanal craft. Like so many garden plants, such as sweet peas and iris, they had their heyday in the early 20th century. Clubs such as the American Primrose, Primula, and Auricula Society were formed and published a quarterly journal. Specialty fertilizer companies advertising secret formulas of whale-based food (the now-defunct Blue Whale brand) boasted prize-winning primula results. In 1936, Florence Bellis, a primrose enthusiast and breeder, founded a tiny nursery called Barnhaven, where she could sell primrose strains developed after years of hand-pollinating. Today, Barnhaven is a name synonymous with premium primroses, and Florence Bellis's genetic strains continue to be

Polyanthus primroses at what is considered the world's premier primrose nursery, but perhaps the only one still breeding them is Barnhaven primroses in Plestin-les-Grèves, France. Seeds or plants can be ordered from their website. Photo by Lee Nelson

hand bred, even though the nursery stock and its name have now moved overseas to France. Barnhaven primroses continue to be the go-to source among enthusiasts for seed and for plants, still shipping to North America as of this printing and offering new strains and species almost every year.

While most species are described by botanists as challenging, at best, to grow as garden plants, a good dozen are very growable and lend themselves to cultivation in our gardens with little effort. The easiest are the species *Primula vulgaris*, *P. veris*, and *P. elatior* for most gardens with average soil and conditions. The complex hybrid commonly known as the polyanthus (*Primula × polyanthus*) combines the genetics of all three of these species. Polyanthus types can come to us two ways, with stalks and flowers set on the end more like an auricula, or newer hybrids that forego the stalk through clever breeding so that the flowers sit upon short pedicels, making the 4-inch (10-cm) pot look more like a brightly colored African violet than anything else. We are likely to see these sold in midwinter just after Christmas (and then we watch them dry to a crisp long before February).

Old timers like me remember the once-popular long-stalked polyanthus. In fact, they may have been the most common primrose of the early 20th century in gardens but have fallen out of favor. In my opinion these stalked polyanthus are still the finest primroses to grow, if not the showiest in a garden setting. They will have umbels of flowers set upon a sturdy stalk (like many of the Barnhaven introductions available today), but to get these, you will need to look hard, order plants from Barnhaven or start your own plants from seed and frequently divide them.

We can get caught up with the Latin here, but it can be very confusing, even for the experts. To simplify things a bit, the words *polyanthus* and *acaulis*, while they sound like Latin names for species, are not. Polyanthus is a relic from pre-Victorian growers, and acaulis is a word that in botanical Latin means "without a stem." Acaulis primroses are just polyanthus varieties that have the habit (stemless flowers) and the look of the wild *P. vulgaris*—a pale-yellow and much beloved primrose in England. As all polyanthus types are complex hybrids, you may see the modern strains sold either as *P. elatior* hybrids, *P. vulgaris* hybrids, or

P. acaulis, as well as specially selected named strains that have unique characteristics, such as the 'Wanda' hybrids. To most people, they all look the same.

Looking back a hundred years, it was practical for local growers to specialize in just one genus. Primrose culture paired nicely with the lost art of raising biennials and beautiful perennials by hand, from seed. In those days, primroses had everything going for them. The seed could be sown and the plants raised *in situ*, either in the field or kept through their first winter in pots held under glass in cold frames, and most local florists and nurseries had cold frames, as did most serious home gardeners. There was no shortage of good, hardy primroses. Well-established plants could be purchased from good nurseries in early spring and set into gardens, where they often became long-loved perennials if tended with biannual division, which is essential. Easy peasy. That is, until modern lifestyles changed everything.

It took only two generations to move primroses from the top of gardeners' wish lists to merely images on teacups and needlepoint pillows at grandma's house. Now it is debatable whether raising primroses in the field makes economic sense for commercial growers, and it is hard to get past the fact that few consumers ask for primroses anymore. Few know about the varieties and species, let alone their names or how to care for them. Long-stemmed polyanthus types have fallen out of favor for short-stemmed or no-stemmed (acaulis) types that look more like African violets than a hardy garden perennial.

In England, there is a long and nostalgic history surrounding the primrose. There the entire primrose fad began in the world's first florists. Today in England, primroses need little explanation, even to nongardeners. In fact, most British can identify the iconic wild *P. vulgaris* (naturalized) and the yellow cowslips (*P. veris*) and oxlips (*P. elatior*) found commonly in hedgerows and woodlands. All three of these make some of the longest-lived and easiest-grown specimens for home gardeners. On the other end of the spectrum are the challenging but highly prized auricula primroses (*P. auricula*), the very same early-blooming primroses once grown in the 1500s in small pots.

THE LANGUAGE OF THE PRIMROSE

Primroses have a long history of human cultivation. Many believe they were the first flowers ever cultivated by mankind, and the term *florist* is even attributed to the primrose. The name "primrose" is rooted in confusion. It comes from *primus*, meaning "first." When combined with *rose*, the flower became known as primrose: the first rose of spring.

Among gardeners, you'll encounter a couple of common synonyms for primrose. *Primula* is the genus name for the primrose. It is a large, diverse genus, and in some ways, it is a more reliable name for the plant type. Today, using the name "primrose" risks confusing the plant with the genus *Oenothera*, or the evening primrose, which is a completely different and unrelated genus. With more than 300 species of *Primula* out there, being as specific as you can is essential.

Polyanthus primroses are the most common, and perhaps most showy, of the common garden primroses. *Polyanthus* is an ancient Greek term meaning "many flowers." Few gardeners refer to the primrose as a polyanthus today, but the term does live on in old literature and routinely appears in Internet searches for primroses, along with a litany of other names that deserve some explanation. Don't expect to find a wild polyanthus; this is a domesticated cross believed to be a mix of at two or three other species (*P. veris, P. elatior,* and *P. vulgaris*).

Polyanthus primrose Barnhaven 'Little Egypt'

GARDEN PRIMROSES YOU CAN GROW

Here is a look at some of the easier-to-grow primroses for most northern, four-season gardeners.

P. DENTICULATA. The drumstick primrose is one worth seeking out at garden centers and nurseries when you can find it. But this early-spring bloomer also can be quickly grown from seed, especially if you buy prechilled seed. Native to the Himalayas, this Asian primrose is unique with its lollypop flower stalk and adds a specific botanical interest to any garden. Remarkably cold hardy, the drumstick primrose can be grown as far north as zone 3. Like most primroses, it emerges just after snowmelt and often blooms alongside the early narcissus and hellebores. Not long-lived if it doesn't get enough spring moisture, it will tolerate regular garden loam but may need refreshing with new seed every few years. I find it easy to grow from seed if I germinate the seeds in a cold frame or greenhouse. A few dollars spent on prechilled seed can result in hundreds of plants, which I set out in midsummer. They will bloom in their second year and look best in their third and fourth year, after which they begin to decline. Biannual division helps keep the clumps vigorous. Plant this species in drifts as they grow in the wild. They love open woodlands with partial sun or other slightly damp, partial-shade areas where they can become the largest specimens.

P. × POLYANTHUS. Sometimes called English primroses, these are hybrids of various species selected for their blooming habit and colors. There are two distinct classes of polyanthus: border and bedding. One can identify these primroses from florist types by their form. Their flowers are carried on an umbel, which sits on a taller stem. The disposable, common florist primroses are caulescent, meaning that each flower sits on its own little stem. Botanically this is known as a peduncle, and we all need a reason to say "peduncle" now and then. They are often sold in winter in small pots for brief indoor color, but buy plants in spring if you plan to plant outdoors.

The native Himalayan primose, *Primula denticulata*, is very cold-hardy. It's often sold as the 'Drumstick Primose.'

'COWICHAN'. This is a distinct strain of the polyanthus primrose that does not have a ringed or distinct eye in the center of the flower. These solid-colored forms were named for a valley in the Pacific Northwest. Their colors could be described as jewel-like, with an attractive dark-tinted foliage when they first emerge in spring.

'GOLD LACE'. A primrose show may display primroses known as 'Gold Lace' primroses, a polyanthus group that is recognized as a distinct group as well. They are highly valued by growers who strive to show off their skill while raising these gold- or silver-edged, blood-red blooms that can look almost artificial with their precise, gold edges.

The old-style Polyanthus primroses make excellent garden plants.

A cowichan-type of polyanthus primrose

Primula 'Gold Laced' group

'JACK IN THE GREEN'. One of the stranger names in the primrose world is the 'Jack in the Green' primrose, sometimes known simply as Jacks. These specimens are double-flowered forms with the addition of a uniquely large green calyx that looks as if it is part of the flower. There are known examples of double Jack in the Green versions of Gold Lace polyanthus primroses.

P. JAPONICA and candelabra. The Japanese candelabra primrose may look fancy and elegant, but given the right conditions, it can be among the easiest to grow. Of course, the right conditions aren't always easy to provide, as these plants crave moisture and thrive on the edges of fast-moving streams, mucky pond-side conditions, or boggy meadows where they can even handle full sun. When given what gardeners often refer to as wet feet, *P. japonica* doesn't just thrive, it spreads and can verge on becoming invasive in some gardens. Candelabra plants are often found in nurseries in the spring and sold to gardeners who unknowingly set the lush rosettes of foliage into their loamy, well-drained perennial borders, where plants may bloom the first year but rarely return. In areas where they thrive, boggy and damp, these plants will self-seed and may continue to populate for decades with little care.

ASIATIC CANDELABRA. Types include *P. florindae*, *P. bulleyana*, *P. × bulleesiana*, *P. pulverentula*, and *P. beesiana*. These are all plants that can be found at specialist online nurseries and may self-seed if happy. While each of these is considered botanically more interesting than the easiest *P. japonica*, there is nothing wrong with easy. Seek out strains with colors you like, such as 'Apple Blossom' with blooms in pale pink or the 'Redfield' strain if you are looking for colors ranging from white to raspberry.

Primula x bulleesiana (a cross between *P. bulleyana* and *P. beesiana*) is one of prettiest of the candellabra primroses.

P. SIEBOLDII. Rarely seen outside of collector gardens, this Japanese native is perfect for woodland gardens that are not dressed with wood mulch. Looking more like woodland phlox than other primroses do, this is a plant that is easy to please and spreads when happy growing in natural leaf mold. In Japan collectors are fanatic about *P. sieboldii*. There are so many named varieties in Japan that it's hard to keep track of them all, yet *P. sieboldii* may be the one primrose even enthusiasts have never heard of in the West, as it remains relatively unknown.

In the garden, *P. sieboldii* is a primrose that likes open woodland conditions, similar to those favored by bloodroot, trillium, and other spring ephemerals, which are all good companions for it. It's rather fleeting, emerging early in spring and blooming a bit later than other woodland plants. It sets seed and disappears underground by early to midsummer.

In Japan *P. sieboldii* is known as Sakurasoh, or cherry blossom primrose. It is much revered and treasured in local shows and displays in villages, where growers display them in pots. In the West, it performs best in the garden. *P. sieboldii* dislikes competition, heavy mulches, or over-fertilizing, preferring shredded leaf mulch and organic matter, or even bare soil, to a crowded planting. It does form colonies though, especially thriving under deciduous trees where the ground is not disturbed once they go dormant.

Easy from seed, most collectors pick the flower stems while the seedpods are still green in late June, and seed production is profuse. Dry the stalks off in a empty vase or bottle. Starting plants from seed is easier than you may think, even though the seed requires chilling or stratification. Seed starting becomes a ritual every winter for enthusiasts who have mastered the technique.

Primula sieboldii remains uncommon in most gardens, and while difficult to find, it is one of the easiest primroses to grow if you have open woodland conditions where it can form large clumps or even seed around.

P. AURICULA. No secret here, *P. auricula* (or simply auriculas, as their fans call them) are challenging to grow, but they are among the most beautiful flowers. When I first attempted growing auriculas, I actually had some luck. While I continue to try a few each year, I am encouraged by some very good friends who have mastered growing them in upstate New York, Vermont, and New Hampshire. While certainly growable, like the other primroses, these are plants that will not tolerate conditions that don't suit them.

Understanding where and how auricula primroses grow in the wild will help you find the perfect spot for them in your garden. Natively they are denizens of the high slopes of the mountains and consequently are perhaps the most winter hardy of all flowering plants. Come summer, they sulk and collapse in hot weather and humidity.

Auriculas love cool, breezy weather. They don't tolerate the freeze/thaw/freeze cycles experienced in lower latitudes. They naturally live where the snow melts quickly in spring in moist, cold alpine meadows, so trying to recreate these conditions at home is key.

Auriculas thrive in glass-covered, open-sided, unheated greenhouses where the outdoor conditions tend to be overcast in winter and dry and bright in the summer. In North America, during winter, most auriculas are kept in sand plunge beds, just above freezing. In Alaska and the far north, auriculas are allowed to freeze solid, and if allowed to thaw and not refreeze in the spring, they will do fine.

The Auricula Theater is a relic of the late 18th century. These structures allowed growers to display their auricula primroses while protecting them from rain which would ruin the white powdery substance (called farina). It appears on the blossoms as well as the foliage on many auricula varieties.

Auriculas have a unique white powdery substance found both on the foliage and sometimes—and most desirably—on the blossoms. This is called "farina" by growers or "paste" when it is found on blossoms. Growing them under the cover of glass or with some protection from rain in the winter and spring will earn you the finest farina. These flowers are about as stunning as a flower can get and can be found in both singles and doubles. The color palette is unmatched in the floral kingdom, ranging from green, white, and true black to gray, silver, mauve, grape, mustard, and true brown, to name a few.

The auricula primroses are organized broadly into two groups: exhibition types and alpine, border auriculas. The showiest are the exhibition types, which generally have the most white farina. These must be protected from direct rain, which will ruin this substance. While exhibition auriculas are the showiest, the easiest of the clan to grow for most people are the border and alpine auriculas. When cultivated outdoors, they can grow into lovely perennial clumps, especially if you garden in the Pacific Northwest. Elsewhere they appreciate alpine garden conditions with excellent drainage yet adequate water and at least 6 hours of direct sun.

If attempting to grow in pots, know that it isn't the cold that hurts these plants but heat and humidity. I've grown great collections in pots that I kept in a small plastic greenhouse (6 × 8 feet [1.8 × 2.4 m]) with the sides removed. Plunged into a raised sand bed in clay pots over the winter, the plants performed well for many years but needed hand watering since rain wasn't allowed to fall on the foliage.

'Stonnel' is one of the many auricula known as 'alpine auriculas'. With no farina and sturdier stems and foliage, the alpine auricula are slightly easier to grow in a well-drained, cool rock garden or in pots in a protected area outdoors if covered from wet rain in the winter or heat and humidity in the summer. Grown by Susan Schnare, a New Hampshire primula enthusiast.

IRIS

Iris spp.

The Iris is apart of one of the botanically rich plant families with over 29 genera and more than 185 taxa, which collectively include well over 1500 species. We are familiar with many of the genera like gladiolus, crocus, ixia, freesia, crocosmia, but the genus iris itself are what most of us think of when we visualize an iris. Just within that genus alone there are at least 300 species, ranging from tiny alpine irises to 5-foot-tall giants.

In our gardens, we generally focus on just a handful of the most impressive and durable species. Many are among the easiest of garden plants, often becoming long-lived heirlooms passed down from generation to generation. Depending on your level of skill and knowledge, growing irises can be practically carefree or intensely challenging.

Iris flowers share some characteristics, most noticeably the three petals (tepals) that often rise upward with three petals typically falling downward. But there are differences, of course,

as garden irises fall into three general groups: bearded irises, Siberian irises, and Japanese irises. A smaller fourth group includes the relatively petite rock garden and woodland irises (*I. cristata* types and other species of tiny iris) that are great for rock gardens.

Taxonomists are continually reevaluating the genus, splitting even the genus *Iris* into smaller groups or reassigning plants of a formerly different genus such as the blackberry lily (once known to gardeners as belamcanda) into what botanists now know as *I. domestica*. Iris enthusiasts and botanists have organized the genus into a hierarchal yet confusing array of horticultural terminology. You will encounter this if you attempt to source an iris from an iris society or a fine specialty catalog. While you don't really need to know the specifics of such vernacular as subgenera, group, divisions, series, and sections, it will help to at least know the very basics.

◀ The heirloom grape-scented iris—*I. pallida* 'Dalmatica' in the author's garden comes from the former Yugoslavia and was long cultivated for the fragrance industry in Tuscany.

BEARDED IRIS

The bearded iris (sometimes improperly referred to as German bearded iris) are the irises most gardeners are familiar with. They have big, blousy, old-fashioned blooms on plants with wide, sword-shaped leaves. Most are tall, but they represent a wide range of heights. The American Iris Society has divided the bearded iris into groups that can seem confusing, but knowing their acronyms is helpful because specialist grower catalogs use the classifications.

The bearded iris groups are:

- Miniature dwarf bearded (MDB), a dwarf bearded iris at 8 inches (20 cm) tall.

- Standard dwarf bearded (SDB), a very useful size for many gardens, at 8 to 16 inches (20 to 40 cm) tall.

- Intermediate bearded (IB) are 16 to 17 inches (40 to 43 cm) tall, with nice branching and interesting colors.

- Border bearded (BB) are really just shorter versions of tall bearded (TB), along with their ruffled flowers and branching. They are around 16 to 17 inches (40 to 43 cm) tall.

- Miniature tall bearded (MTB), a 16- to 27-inch (40- to 69-cm)–tall iris with a wiry stem that makes them popular with floral designers and garden designers.

- Tall bearded (TB) are up to a stately 30 inches (76 cm) in height with the largest flowers and thickest stems.

Many bearded irises are fragrant, with scents like grape soda or root beer, and have a color range that is truly fantastic. Their popularity may be limited by the fact that they don't do well in pots and bloom for only a few weeks. Finding suitable specimens can also be difficult. You can find bearded irises in a cardboard box in early spring but seldom in suitable varieties. Occasionally you'll find a 1-gallon (3.8-L) plant at a nursery, and you can order bearded irises in the spring for summer planting in July, August, or September. If you

This standard Dwarf Bearded Iris has been growing in our garden for at least three generations. The name is long lost, but its nearly black petals always gets comments from visitors.

are serious about sourcing some amazing and viable bearded iris stock, your best bet is a website or a catalog from an iris grower. Avoid ordering cardboard tubes containing a plastic bag with a dormant rhizome or, worse yet, a slip that has begun to grow. These rarely will grow well, and if they do, they are likely inferior varieties.

GROWING BEARDED IRISES

Planting iris rhizomes can be intimidating for new gardeners, as it seems that they should be planted halfway deep—a common mistake. The entire rhizome should be underground but barely covered with soil. Dig a trench about 4 inches (10 cm) deep with a slightly raised portion running down the center. Position the rhizome on that raised portion and allow the roots, if any, to drape into the soil deeper around the trench. Fill in with soil but leave the top of the rhizome exposed. Rain may erode a bit of the soil off the top. Be sure to firm the soil in tightly to ensure that the roots begin to grow downward.

A bearded iris rhizome needs to hold a tremendous amount of weight when mature because it has a floral scape that can be nearly a yard (1 m) tall. Space multiple rhizomes or fans about a 1½ feet (45 cm) apart. A grouping of at least five to seven plants will create the best effect in the garden. You will notice that bearded irises creep along the ground in a particular direction (usually south); it is recommended to position new fans all facing in the same direction to create the most natural effect.

Bearded irises should be divided and replanted in midsummer, about 5 or 6 weeks after they have bloomed. If dividing mature plants, look for clumps that are at least 3 or 4 years old and check to see if they are declining in the center of the clumps. Dig the entire clump up a month or two after the plant has bloomed. Any later and the iris rhizomes won't have enough time to form the deep contractile roots that help the plant hold firmly in the soil through the winter. Carefully remove the healthiest fans from the clump by gingerly snapping them off or by cutting them with a knife. Save only the 6 to 8 inches (15 to 20 cm) that are newest, always with a large fan of foliage. Wash off the roots and cut the foliage into a pointed fan shape, leaving about 6 to 8 inches (15 to 20 cm) of the leaf.

Planting a division of a hybrid bearded Iris in late summer.

Some bearded irises are rebloomers (they put forth a second bloom in the fall). If you have this type, wait a few years after planting before you divide them so you do not interrupt their late-summer bloom. Plant newly arrived fans once they arrive in the mail in summer or after you have dug and divided your plants every 4 years.

Bearded irises appreciate a balanced, slow-release fertilizer that is lower in nitrogen, such as bonemeal. Dig in bonemeal 10 inches (25 cm) deep before planting, and then apply a few times during the summer growing months. Site bearded irises in sunny, well-drained spots, adding sand if you have clay soil.

SIBERIAN IRIS

Siberian irises are sturdy garden plants, and most of us know of the older purple strains often passed down from our grandmothers' gardens. They offer everything good about irises. They are sturdy and long-lived, with a longer blooming period in the garden as many buds form on their long stems. The foliage remains green and attractive until hard frost. The Siberians are more resilient and less bothered by disease and insects than other iris types, and their stems never need to be staked. They need to be divided less often, usually once the center of the clump begins to die out and open up. One established, Siberian iris clumps can be divided into a dozen plants or more every 5 years or so.

What really makes Siberian irises sing in the garden is their color, especially the newer selections that have expanded beyond the primarily blue, white, purple, and yellow of older varieties. They are perfect border plants for perennial gardens, but they are difficult to find in stores.

Iris sibirica, 'Art in Bloom'

JAPANESE IRIS

You'll rarely see the Japanese *Iris ensata* in modern gardens, but you'll recognize them if you've ever seen a Japanese screen. Outside of Japan, where it is frequently planted in pots, the Japanese iris seems to suffer from the same negative of blooming too late for nurseries to feature them, as few shop for perennial plants in late June or July when they bloom. They flower about a month after the tall bearded iris, closer to the time the first true lilies bloom. Many people may overlook them at nurseries, as they look more like cattails or tall Siberian irises with no flower buds showing yet. Of all the irises, the Japanese iris has perhaps the most architectural appearance and is able to stand alone in the garden as a specimen plant.

Although screens and woodblock prints often showed Japanese irises growing along streams, it is a common mistake to actually plant them along a stream or pond.

These are not water irises. For that, you may want to plant *I. pseudacorus*, the yellow flag iris, or another iris that appreciates growing in water. Be warned that though *I. pseudacorus* has temptingly tall foliage, it is considered an invasive plant in North America. Japanese irises grow best in good, rich, well-drained garden loam. If planting near water or a stream, position them higher on a bank to ensure that their feet don't get wet.

Japanese iris displays benefit when planted in sweeps or drifts. They are slow to form clumps that can be divided, so it is best to buy five to seven to set out 2 feet (0.61 m) apart, either in a garden bed or in a lawn. They look lovely this way.

Japanese irises produce large flowers. Their color palette is limited to shades of purple and reddish violet to pure white and lavender. Like Siberian irises, their foliage is attractive until frost, and because it is more statuesque, it can be a statement plant in the landscape.

Japanese iris (*I. ensata*) bloom later than most other garden iris species. They grow best in acidic soil that remains moist all summer, but they don't like to grow submerged in water.

LILAC

Syringa spp.

Lilac shrubs are so commonplace in many parts of North America that it may surprise you to learn that they are not native to this continent. Of the 20 species of lilacs, 2 come from Europe and 18 from Asia. While not native to North American, lilacs were fragrant imports that arrived around the same time as the colonists. Today, lilacs are one of the first plants young families choose to grow when they get their first homes.

Although deliciously fragrant and beautiful when in bloom, lilac shrubs rarely make an excellent specimen plant and are best if located somewhere they can grow tall. They can (and should) be picked as cut flowers. They are not well suited for use as hedges or clipped shrubs.

Lilacs are stunningly beautiful when in bloom, but it is the unmistakable scent of the blossoms that is behind much of the lilac's appeal. It is as signature as any French perfume.

REGENERATING OLD LILACS

Pruning is critical with old lilacs, and while many choose to prune an ancient, woody lilac in early spring, this is the wrong time. Prune an old lilac just after it blooms. Either remove all the dead and mature growth down to the ground, leaving 10-inch (25-cm) stumps, or cut limbs with a saw, removing about one-third of the old growth each year until the entire shrub is regenerated. Amend the soil with a balanced fertilizer like a 10-10-10 or manure, and add plenty of ground limestone to the surface. Keep an eye on watering as well, applying an inch (2.5 cm) a week as a good target. Expect new growth to bloom in the second year after pruning.

◀ Pale pink Lilac 'Marie Frances'

LILAC SPECIES AND HYBRIDS

There are many lilac varieties and hybrids to choose from, but if you are looking for pure lilac fragrance, look for *Syringa vulgaris*. Other varieties, such as Korean lilac may be highly scented, but the fragrance is nothing you'd identify as lilac. Korean lilac has strong scents of jasmine or spicy viburnum, which is still lovely but may be disappointing if you're expecting that classic lilac scent. In addition to fragrance of bloom, color and form vary among lilacs and should be taken into account.

S. VULGARIS and *S. VULGARIS × HYACINTHIFLORA*. With more than 150 named cultivars, the choices in this group are beyond numerous. For fragrance, look for hybrids created from *S. vulgaris* or *S. × hyacinthiflora*, which is a hybrid made from *S. vulgaris* and *S. oblata*. These are the most common fragrant lilacs found in the trade today. They are practically unidentifiable from pure *S. vulgaris* cultivars, except that according to the Arnold Arboretum, the holder of North America's largest and oldest collection of lilacs, the *S. × hyacinthiflora* crosses bloom earlier.

S. MEYERI 'Palibin'. This award-winning Meyer lilac, sometimes sold incorrectly as a dwarf Korean lilac, is exceptional and has many excellent characteristics, including low, dense growth and good disease resistance. It's native to China, with sweetly scented small heads of flowers in spring.

S. PEKINENSIS Morton 'China Snow'. An award-winning tree lilac, this selection is genuinely worthy as a shade or street tree with plumes of yellowish-white fragrant flowers in early summer and sensational glossy red and peeling bark, much like a cherry tree.

S. PROTOLACINATA. The Afghan lilac is worth seeking out for its dissected and unique foliage that gives it a different but landscape-worthy look. Fragrant.

Lilac syringa 'Charles Joly'. Photo Credit: Kate Wollensak Freeborn

Lilac Bloomerang. Photo Credit: Kate Wollensak Freeborn

S. PUBESCENS subsp. **PATULA.** This popular Korean lilac is commonly found in nurseries, usually under the cultivar name 'Miss Kim.' Strongly fragrant with a spicy *Viburnum carlesii* scent reminiscent of cloves and cinnamon.

S. RETICULATA 'Ivory Silk'. This Japanese tree lilac looks more like a heptacodium than it does a lilac, but is a choice small flowering tree. It has a musky fragrance that is not for everyone.

S. VILLOSA 'Charles Hepburn'. The Russian lilac is sometimes known as the late lilac, as it blooms late compared to other lilacs. Its pale, pink flowers are fragrant and look like Korean lilac. It makes an excellent hedge plant that can be trimmed.

PLANTING NEW LILACS

Lilacs are best grown in an area of the garden that can handle their casual form. Often they are included in a loose hedgerow of shrubs or set along the boundary of a yard. A well-grown lilac naturally looks untidy.

Planting a young lilac couldn't be easier. There are plenty of varieties available today, both old and new. As with many plants, the more modern strains tend to be more vigorous and disease resistant. Resist buying value plants from mail-order sources that promise a bare-root lilac shrub for just a few dollars. These may take years to establish themselves, and even when they do, the results are often not satisfactory.

Starting with a nursery-bought 1- to 5-gallon (3.8- to 19-L) container is best. Prepare a hole with soil that is slightly acidic to alkaline—lilacs love a slightly alkaline soil (7.0 pH). A little horticultural powdered lime will make soil more alkaline if your soil tends to be acidic. Lilacs also dislike drought and do best with about an inch (2.5 cm) of water a week. Remember, they form their flower buds in late summer, often when droughts are at their peak, so additional irrigation is helpful.

PRUNING LILACS

Lilacs are loosely growing shrubs, and while long-lived, they do need some annual maintenance if you want the best possible blooms. There is a proper way to prune lilacs and plenty of wrong ways. The right way is to remove one-third of the old trunks once a shrub has matured and has woody, bark-covered trunks. Lilacs bloom best on newer branches, usually ones that rise from the base and are 2 to 3 years old. Old, mature wood will form small, thin limbs, and while flower buds will still form, the weight of the flowers is often too much for the spindly stems, and the flower heads will be much smaller.

Removing old woody stems from mature plants is best done after the flowers have faded, usually in late June. This will give the plant time for new stems to emerge from the base of the shrub. By removing one-third every year, you will continue to get some bloom every year. Some older shrubs may benefit from complete removal of all large stems at once, but blooms may stop for a couple of years until growth is mature again.

DISEASES AND PESTS

Lilacs are most prone to powdery mildew damage, which can be controlled with copper-based sprays. Often this affliction doesn't harm flower buds, as it appears late in summer. Powdery mildew typically appears in midsummer as a white, powdery substance on the surface of the leaves. Proper pruning to thin shrubs and a breezy site will help.

◀ Lilacs bloom best with heavy biannual pruning, so why not be more aggressive while cutting blooms for arrangements? This bucket of cut branches adds a classic New England touch to a Woodstock, Vermont terrace.

SUMMER BLOOMS

Here in New England, summer can really be divided into three distinct seasons. Early summer can be every bit as variable and unpredictable as spring. It is often cool and rainy, but it will just as likely be sunny and hot. High summer tends to be more stable, marked by heat and sun and vigorous growth. When late summer arrives, growth slows and the first yellowing leaves appear as nights grow longer and cooler. At the same time, new crops of flowers emerge in each season according to their growth patterns and preferences.

As much as gardeners seem to love to complain about the weather, weather always plays a key role in the success of a garden. Of course, we have no control over it, but we do have control over what we choose plant or sow, and when. We celebrate summer with flowers everywhere, whether for picking for arrangements or leaving alone in borders as landscape enhancement.

Adventurous gardeners are optimistic. We stubbornly try to grow flowers a zone or two warmer or the other way around, hoping for that perfectly long and cool spring that lasts into summer or a summer with adequate rainfall and low humidity. We then discover later that droughts and heat waves were the reality.

Setting the weather aside, summer is the peak season for flowers, regardless of where you live. CSAs and flower farms share their bounty at farmers markets, and our own gardens bear us floral gifts almost every day. Savvy gardeners often can tell the exact date by what is in bloom in their garden. The season may begin with cool-loving, rarer annuals like larkspurs, schizanthus, and viscaria, which must be raised from direct-sown seed. The dependable flowers of midsummer often are the more familiar perennials. Popular again are zinnias, asters, and marigolds, heat-loving annuals that are easy to grow from seed sown in early summer. And of course there are the majestic border bulbs like lilies and dahlias to enjoy.

◀ A summer without zinnias is like a summer without ice cream. Plant rows, just for cutting, in the vegetable garden every three weeks until mid-August for continual blooms.

ABOVE: *Salpiglossis sinuata* 'Kew Blue'

RIGHT: New agapanthus varieties are being introduced with increasing frequency, like this bicolored variety 'Twister'

LEFT: Shirley poppies are one of the most beautiful and delicate of annuals. Fragile and a bit challenging to grow, its flowers like this that make them so desirable.

ABOVE: Intersectional or Orient Pet lilies are sometimes sold as 'tree lilies' as they grow stems that are stronger than traditional selections, but most will still need staking as these can reach heights taller than 6 feet (1.8 m).

ABOVE: Dahlia 'Hollyhill Calico' a miniature ball but grown on a plant that can reach 6 feet (1.8 m) tall. Some are completely red while others are all ivory with just a speck of color on one petal.

RIGHT: A mouthful to pronounce, Zaluzianskya or Night Phlox looks understated and is often best grown in containers, as one grows not just for its appearance but for its vanilla scent at night.

LEFT: Mignonette (*Reseda odorata*) are about as old fashioned as one can get when it comes to growing annuals. It was a popular Victorian cut flower, but rarely seen or grown anymore. Their fragrance, while mild, is not unlike that of scented violets.

ABOVE: Nicotiana collection in vases. Clockwise from top: Fragrant *Nicotiana longiflora*, *N. knightiana*, *N. alata* 'Tinkerbell,' and *N. langsdorffii*, which self seeds beautifully around the garden.

LAVENDER

Lavandula spp.

Lavender grows best in alkaline soil, enjoying a pH between 6.8 and 7.0. It enjoys plenty of water but requires good drainage too. It will not tolerate continually wet conditions in the summer or poor drainage combined with freezing winter conditions. Lavender performs exceptionally well in California, Colorado, and the western mountain states, but with some attention, it can be coaxed to success in most growing areas. See Featured Flower, page 157.

- Lavender likes sandy soil where water drains freely.

- Plant in full sun. The more hours per day lavender gets sunshine, the better.

- Lavender struggles in rich, acidic soil, growing best in slightly alkaline soil with a pH between 6.5 and 7.5.

- Variety matters. Choose the right variety for your region.

AGAPANTHUS
Agapanthus spp.

Agapanthus are as sturdy as hostas or daylilies, but they can be fussy when it comes to blooming. Plants in the amaryllis family, including clivia and amaryllis, are easier to raise if you avoid root damage and keep frost away from the roots and inner stems. While commercially propagated varieties now appear in many of our gardens and are worth seeking out, new named selections are often better choices, as some can reach 5 feet (1.5 m) tall and have flower heads over a foot (30 cm) across. Any agapanthus variety is a valuable addition to the garden.

- If it is your first season with an agapanthus, plant it in a very large pot or tub (14 inches [36 cm] or larger) and keep it well watered and fertilized.

- A heavy feeder, agapanthus appreciates high nitrogen in spring, but choose an N-P-K plant food higher in phosphorus and potassium if you want flower buds to form during the summer. Agapanthus form embryonic flower buds in the summer that will bloom the following year.

- Bring plants in after the first frost in autumn and store them in a cool cellar or a sunroom until spring. Agapanthus in the north have long been considered conservatory plants worthy of keeping from year to year in a cold room or greenhouse.

WISTERIA
Wisteria spp.

PEONY
Paeonia spp.

Wisteria is a woody flowering plant that can become an architectural focal point in your garden. Look for a variety that flowers before the foliage matures and is a profuse bloomer so it will cover a trellis or arbor with its long, graceful trusses. Make a plan for staking and pruning your wisteria, then stick to it. See Featured Flower, page 163.

- Trim back long whips and aggressive growth in midsummer.
- Cut back aggressive or inappropriate growth in late autumn.
- Remove seedpods at any time.

Peonies have many flower types, from single-flowered blooms with a big boss of yellow stamens to semidoubles and doubles. Flowers that have a row of single petals around a dense pompom in the center are known as a "bomb" peonies by peony growers. There are also many novelties ranging from mutated ones with twisted, thin petals to those with entirely green flowers. See Featured Flower, page 149. As for garden varieties, there are many that are excellent cut flowers but only a few that are considered useful landscape plants.

- Peony color is affected by both soil and light, so take notes on each variety that you grow.
- Regional differences are commonly based upon soil chemistry.
- A variety like 'Coral Charm' can have a brilliant coral color when it first opens, but indoors it will fade to a buff color.

COSMOS

Cosmos bipinnatus, C. sulphureus

Cosmos are ridiculously easy to grow if sown directly or outdoors in early summer in individual cells. Most problems with cosmos occur when plants are sown too early indoors, with nursery-grown plants that were treated with plant growth regulators. Cosmos diversity has expanded over the past decade, and flowers of many styles, types, and color can be found. There should be no hurry to start cosmos seed, as waiting until summer has fully arrived will solve all of your problems. Sow seed outdoors in individual pots, one per pot, or directly in the soil. Grown this way, cosmos will reach their fullest potential.

- Sow seed late using named varieties.
- Cover seeds lightly and water well.
- Thin the rows but do not transplant, as root disturbance stunts future growth.
- Always direct sow, then this the rows but do not transplant, as root disturbance stunts future growth.
- Successive sowings every few weeks until early August will ensure consistent blooms of high quality for cutting.

MARIGOLD

Tagetes spp.

Marigolds are definitely a love-them-or-hate-them flower. Like other annuals, such as zinnia and cosmos, we often fall into the trap of starting our marigolds too early indoors. Direct-sown seeds in early summer will always outgrow and outperform any store-bought seedling. With marigolds, as with zinnias, you can cheat and sow seed into cells or modules outdoors in late spring to get a jump on things. Be conscious about roots getting too tightly bound in their containers, however, as the best plants come when roots are allowed to grow freely.

- Sow marigold seeds outside in early summer or start early 4 weeks in advance of the soil reaching 65°F (18°C).
- While they can transplant well, take care not to damage roots for the healthiest plants.
- Look for tall heirloom varieties as well as interesting selections in specialty catalogs.

ASTER

Callistephus chinensis

While most of the annual species in the genus *Aster* were assigned to the genus *Callistephus* years ago, as far as most home gardeners go, they remain known as asters. Our grandmothers knew them better as China asters. Despite their ongoing rise in popularity, they are not as easy to grow as you might think. If you have experienced failures with asters, one reason may be that you bought seedlings that were too old. The best results come from seedlings raised at home at the right time and transplanted carefully without any stress. They do even better if direct-sown in June or early July and thinned, never transplanted.

- Sow seed later, in May or June.
- Sow in cells individually and keep bright.
- Transplant carefully to minimize root disturbance.
- Plants are prone to fungus. The best crops are isolated from other plants, such as in a row in the vegetable garden.

ZINNIA

Zinnia elegans

Zinnias have emerged, along with dahlias, as one of the most popular flowers today. If you've struggled with zinnias in the past, know that the best crops come from seeds sown directly once summer has arrived and the soil is warm. Transplanted plants will never perform as well, regardless of where you got them. Flower farmers know that zinnias can be succession sown right up until early August, with the best crops coming from later sowing.

- Sow all annual species later in the season.
- Use a sterile soil mix if starting in cells and grow them in full sun outside if possible.
- Transplant cells carefully as root disturbance will affect their performance.
- Most zinnia problems happen because store-bought plants are already rootbound.
- Zinnias respond well to high fertility. Use plenty of compost and keep well irrigated.

AMARANTHUS
Amaranthus caudatus

ST. JOSEPH'S COAT
Amaranthus tricolor

AT-A-GLANCE

The chenille plant, commonly called Love Lies Bleeding, is perhaps the oddest looking annual. A centerpiece in many famous Victorian gardens, amaranths have found a new audience to enjoy the unique beauty of these cascading dreadlocks, which come in both green and red forms. Always best when direct-sown, plants can easily be had if one sows seed at home outdoors in cell containers in early June. Speedy growth comes with heat, humidity, and no root disturbance. Plants can reach 7 feet (2 m) tall if fed and watered well in fertile soil. We all learn the hard way with amaranthus, that one seed that self-sows and was never transplanted will grow the tallest and be twice as impressive as any sown in pots.

- Start carefully in individual cells, keeping the conditions warm and bright.

- Transplant carefully to avoid root disturbance.

- Maintain high fertility and stake plants, as they will become tall and heavy.

Also known as summer poinsettia (as well as other varietal names based on the color selection), *Amaranthus tricolor* is one of the oldest amaranths cultivated and, with several selected forms, offers a color for any taste. By far the most colorful is this one pictured, grown even in Colonial times. The color palette, while not to everyone's taste, is undeniably summery. Rarely seen in gardens today, the best displays come from seeds that were direct-sown, which is tricky due to the tiny seed. Starting seedlings individually in cells works best if you take great care in transplanting before the roots reach the bottom.

- Amaranths like heat and humidity; avoid cold soil and sow late.

- Look for other strains and selections with single colors.

AMARANTHUS HYBRIDUS
Amaranthus hybridus

The amaranth family has its share of thugs and do-gooders, and it is enjoying a resurgence in popularity. A Victorian and Edwardian favorite, new breeding strategies are introducing many new cultivars to accompany some old selections. Along with the popularity of the pseudo-grain quinoa, also an amaranth, the entire plant is edible, from seed to stem. But it is as a cut flower or a spectacular garden plant that the amaranth excels.

- Start seed carefully in individual cells 4 weeks before setting out, after frost threats have passed.

- Amaranths enjoy warm soil and air (higher than 70°F [21°C]) so don't expect fast growth until the summer heat arrives.

- High fertility and adequate moisture are essential.

- Stake tall plants before they tumble.

- Plants can self-seed, and these volunteers will often be taller and more robust than those in the previous year.

CELOSIA
Celosia caudatus, Celosia argentea

Closely related to the amaranths, celosia is also experiencing a rise in popularity, especially given the growing popularity of the slow-flower movement. It is best if grown in a cut-flower garden, where it can grow tall and be cut to the base when needed for arrangements. Celosia shares many of the same traits and cultural requirements as amaranth. Look for various forms like cockscombs, brain-like coral flower heads, or plume-like varieties.

- Start seed early under lights, kept warm (70°F [21°C]). The plant can handle transplanting while young, but sowing individually in plug trays is best.

- Set out plugs once soil has fully warmed, and use a plastic mulch to keep weeds down.

- Celosia loves heat, so resist setting plants out too early in summer.

AT-A-GLANCE

CLARKIA (GODETIA)

Clarkia spp.

CLARKIA

How could anyone not want to grow clarkia? These salmon-colored flowers look even more delicate than poppies but are easier to grow, and they deserve a place in any garden. Once known as godetia, clarkia is a native North American genus that was named after Captain William Clark of the Lewis and Clark expedition. While the once-common name godetia continues to be used by many seed catalogs and growers, it's probably best to get used to calling it by its proper name to avoid confusion.

Most clarkia species will take about 3 months to bloom from seed, so an early start is helpful, either indoors under lights or directly in the ground. Light freezes seem to do little harm. Never sow seeds in a flat, but plant them individually in small cells or a few seeds per 2- to 3-inch (5- to 8-cm) pot, removing all but one to avoid transplanting.

- Most clarkias sold today are complex hybrids of *Clarkia unguiculata*, *C. elegans*, and *C. pulchella*. These produce the showiest and largest flowers of the 33 species known.

- All clarkia species resent hot and humid weather, but seedlings set out into the garden in late April or early May can bloom through June and July before succumbing to the heat.

Of western American wildflowers, clarkia may be the showiest, given its desirable color palette of primarily coral and pink shades and its long bloom period. With the recent appreciation of native plants and pollinator flowers, many adventurous gardeners are rediscovering the species of clarkia, and many varieties are now becoming available from specialty seed catalogs.

Massed together, clarkia has a distinctive presence. I find that the best results come from seedlings that I have raised in the cold greenhouse.

Pinch seedlings once or twice to stimulate branching lower on the stalk. Otherwise, you may end up with a 24-inch (60-cm) stem and one head of flowers at the end. Transplant young plants to their final location while the weather is still cold, before the roots begin to emerge from the bottoms of their pots. Space 6 to 8 inches (15 to 20 cm) apart. Clarkia makes good cut flowers, lasting at least 4 days in a vase, and some secondary buds may open to extend the bloom. In the garden, deadheading the old flower heads (the ones with long seedpods) will help prolong the bloom. Species in the *clarkia elegans* group include the following:

- *C. amoena* 'Memoria'. White satin flowers with blushy-pink bases to each petal. Good cut flower.

- *C. concinna* 'Pink Ribbons'. Delicate species with cloud-like displays of fringed flowers. Shiny, red stems.

- *C. elegans*. Long known as farewell-to-spring or godetia. Tall stems with small flowers that look like tufts of pink tissue. Good for containers or winter greenhouse culture too.

- *C. pulchella* 'Snowflake'. Uniquely cut petals that look like white snowflakes. Easy to grow.

- *C. pulchella* 'Double Choice Mix'. Tall spikes that can look like larkspurs. Good for cutting. Comes in all the pastel pink shades.

- *C. purpurea* 'Burgundy Wine'. A named cultivar of the Californian species with small but lovely dark burgundy flowers and bluish foliage.

GLOBE AMARANTH
Gomphrena globosa

STRAWFLOWER
Helichrysum spp.

The globe amaranth seemed to arrive from nowhere, yet its rise in popularity is a testament to how an old-fashioned annual can make a colossal comeback practically overnight. Widespread in gardens during the late 1700s and 1800s, its popularity as a bedding plant on large estates fell out of fashion as styles changed. By the mid–20th century, its use was primarily limited to that of a novelty dried flower. In the past 20 years, everything changed, as designers and gardeners discovered the merits of a sturdy annual that could grow tall and be ever-blooming. Even in a drought, the natural-looking gomphrena performs beautifully. Today there is a gomphrena for most every style, from dwarf, dense-growing miniatures to tall, natural, and wild-looking varieties in almost every color within the pink, white, and purple range.

- Gomphrena is easy from seed if the soil is kept warm.

- Transplant easily into the garden around the same time you plant tomatoes.

- Seeds should be started indoors, under lights 6-8 weeks before your last frost.

Among the flowers grown mainly for dried floral arrangements, the helichrysum (*Helichrysum bracteatum* and other species) is the most familiar. Yet as a garden plant, its beauty is limited to its floral display and not its foliage. If you plan on picking the flowers to dry, know that the terminal blossom will fade before any side buds open, making for an untidy garden plant. As such, it is best to plant strawflowers somewhere where they can be picked as they open and can be used either as a fresh or dried flower.

- If drying flowers, cut individual blossoms off at midday just as they open, and cut the stem off to the base of the flower. Run a hooked wired down through the center of each flower until the hooked end disappears within the center and allow to dry.

- Helichrysum is easily started from seed sown indoors 4 to 6 weeks before the last frost date.

- Successive sowing until mid-July will extend harvests.

- All the helichrysum species enjoy hot, dry weather and full sun at all times.

PETUNIA
Petunia × *atkinsiana*

MISSION BELLS
Calibrachoa hybrids

Once the darling of the 1950s garden, the common petunia fell out of fashion in the late 20th century, regarded as too common. Fast forward to today, and the petunia is brand new thanks to breeding efforts that have not only transformed the petunia into something more garden worthy but has also made the plant almost unrecognizable to the inferior old forms and colors that our parents had.

- Look for (more expensive) branded hybrid cultivars with patent numbers, as these are the newest, sterile selections that won't produce seed, allowing them to bloom nonstop until frost.

- If raising older varieties from seed, start warm and indoors under lights for 8 to 10 weeks before planting time. Transplant into cells before setting out after all threats of frost.

- Seedling are slow growing at first. If seedings produce yellow leaves, even with nitrogen, consider using a cal-mag fertilizer (often available at hydroponic supply stores.)

- Keep seedpods and old flowers deadheaded for continued bloom, and trim it back in midsummer to extend the show.

Twenty years ago, you would have been hard pressed to find a calibrachoa at a garden center. Most gardeners think they are petunias. While closely related, they are completely different plants. Mostly ever-blooming, the new hybrid calibrachoas have smaller flowers than petunias, and the flowers come in larger quantities. The color palette gets more incredible with every season.

- Few calibrachoas can be started from seed.

- The excellent varieties must be propagated from cuttings or seed that is patented, so always buy plants at a reputable garden center.

- If starting from seed, follow the same cultural guidelines as for petunias.

ANNUAL PHLOX
Phlox drummondii

Phlox is a large genus, with alpines, perennials, and woodland species, but the North American native *Phlox drummondii* is an annual that has been treasured in gardens since the 1800s. Yet by the 1980s, they had nearly disappeared from gardens and seed catalogs. New improvements in breeding over the past 25 years have brought us exciting strains, and we are beginning to find *P. drummondii* tempting us again. Notoriously fussy to grow, newer seed-raised strains are more vigorous and floriferous than older varieties. While able to tolerate transplanting when young, older plants suffer, so thin them wisely.

- Start phlox indoors under lights or under glass.

- Phlox should germinate cool and grow even cooler (45°F to 50°F [7°C to 10°C]).

- Transplanting is easy while seedlings are young, not when they are older.

- In zones 6 and higher, you can direct sow but only if you are a judicious weeder and can identify the small, slow-growing seedlings.

SALPIGLOSSIS (PAINTED TONGUE)
Salpiglossis sinuata

They may look like petunias, but this old-fashioned relative of the tomato is anything but. What often deceives us with salpiglossis are those close-up beauty shots in seed catalogs, as they rarely show the entire plant in its full glory. Its common name, painted tongue, comes from the distinctive pattern on the throat of every flower. Grown for their unique color palette, they include some near-black and maroon flowers that are very close to wild relatives from Chile. A little difficult to raise from seed, you must still resist buying seedlings from a garden center unless they specialize in rare annuals, for even a day too long in a cell pack causes salpiglossis to suffer. The best results will come from seeds that you raise carefully at home.

- Start seeds indoors early, 6 to 8 weeks before planting, in a warm environment.

- Surface-sow seeds thinly in complete darkness to germinate, but do not cover the seed. Instead, cover the seed tray with cardboard or foil until seedlings sprout.

- Set seedlings outdoors in the garden or in large containers once the weather has fully warmed.

BUTTERFLY FLOWER
Schizanthus pinnatus

DIASCIA (TWINSPUR)
Diascia spp.

First described in the late 1700s, schizanthus quickly became common glass-house plants by 1835. At the time, they were grown from wild-collected seed from coastal Chile and Peru. It has since grown to be a treasured annual for cold greenhouses, commonly grown in gardens where summer temperatures remain cool in the evening. Use sterilized soil when panting seed, as the genus is susceptible to fungus. Sow the tiny seed on the surface of damp soil about 10 to 12 weeks before your last frost. Keep light levels bright but cool. Pick off seedlings once they are large enough to handle (they don't mind being transplanted).

- Schizanthus seeds should be surface-sown, as plants need light to germinate.

- Keep seed trays and plants cool at all times (50°F to 60°F [10°C to 16°C]).

- A biweekly feed with a low-nitrogen fertilizer helps schizanthus maintain strength.

- This plant grows better in pots and containers than in the garden.

This relative of the snapdragon is commonly found along with other cool-spring growing annuals like pansies, mimulus, and nemesia (to which it is most closely related). All share similar cultural needs once planted in the garden or containers, enjoying the cool weather of spring. They fade once the weather turns hot in summer. They all fill a gap that once could only be filled with spring bulbs or pansies.

- Look for new, patented selections at garden centers in early spring. They have been grown from cuttings and are more vigorous than seed-raised strains.

- Combine diascia in containers with spring bulbs or other early flowers.

- Expect to replace them once the weather turns hot in summer, or cut back plants for rebloom in cool climates.

- Seeds germinate easily if fresh and if surface-sown. They need light to germinate.

- Grow in cool (60°F [16°C]) temperatures in bright light and harden off, as young plants are more sensitive to cold. Pinch regularly to promote branching.

ACROCLINIUM

Rhodanthe chlorocephala subsp. *rosea*

Often sold under many names, from pink paper daisy to acroclinium, rhodanthe is the current accepted name (though most seed catalogs still list acroclinium). A native Australian plant, rhodanthe blossoms look and behave very much like strawflowers, but they look good when planted in a garden, as they produce multiple graceful stems topped off with a single blossom. The only downside is getting them to open when garden visitors arrive—it takes full sun.

Sited near a path or in a rock garden, the 1- to 2-foot (30- to 60-cm) plants form graceful gooseneck stems that each sport a strawflower daisy. Available in many shades of white, pink, or dark rose, rhodanthe is not as commonly grown as helichrysum but as a border plant it performs much nicer, forming dense colonies with wiry stems 1½ foot (0.45 m) tall never requiring staking. Plant in large groups and seek out single-color strains for the best garden effect.

- Start seeds early indoors or under glass in cold (60°F [16°C]) temperatures. Cover seed lightly and water well. Transplants easily.

- Rhodanthe transplants easily, but it can be direct-sown as well.

- Plant in borders in large swaths for best effect.

MIMULUS (MONKEY FLOWER)

Erythranthe spp. and hybrids

Mimulus are not demanding, but you need to know they like and don't like. All enjoy cool (if not cold) temperatures and wet feet. Most species grow in puddles or near streams in mountainous areas.

The surprise here is that erythranthe (the new botanical name for mimulus, but I dare you to find it listed as that) is very easy to grow from seed. They are quick to bloom, and as they enjoy cold weather at every stage of their growth (from seed germination to maturity), they are great for northern gardeners. Elsewhere, they can be adapted to grow most of the summer, even in warm and humid climates if you grow them in containers. They can be planted as early as pansies, as they are able to withstand light frost. In summer heat, they can be plunged into trays of water to soak them and keep them cool.

- Numerous new varieties are being introduced, and interspecific crosses are making mimulus the next calibrachoa.

- Start seeds early indoors on a cool windowsill or porch, and transplant into larger pots, pinching plants once they have their third set of leaves.

NEMESIA

Nemesia spp. and hybrids

The cool-loving nemesia is an annual that boasts many new cultivars every year. Many are sterile (plants that even when pollinated don't produce seed), which extends their bloom period longer into early summer. This trait makes nemesia even more desirable, both as a bedding plant and as a container plant. These new strains are vegetatively propagated (grown from cuttings rather than seeds), thus ensuring perfect clones that make new named varieties patentable and profitable. Often sold under brands like Proven Winners or Suntory, both have developed their own unique strains, and more are sure to follow from other breeders.

Nemesia will only become more popular as gardeners try and use them as they were intended to be used: as a replacement for other early spring annuals, particularly pansies. They grow best in bright light, and a temperature between 65°F and 75°F (18°C to 24°C) during the day, with about a 10-degree differential at night. These cooler nights are essential for a long blooming period and help keep the plants tight and compact.

- Nemesia is winter blooming outdoors in zones 9 and 10.

- This plant prefers cool weather at all times.

- Nemesia is challenging to start from seeds without cool greenhouse conditions.

- Nemesia is useful in pots and containers as a substitute for pansies.

TASSEL FLOWER

Emilia coccinea

Emilia may not look like much as first, but when viewed in the garden, its presence transforms a space into a Georges Seurat–style pointillist painting. Wiry stems emerge from what first at may look like weeds but open up into glowing embers on wavy wands that delicately illuminate gardens. Once you grow emilia, you won't want to be without it. Look for the characteristic red or (hard-to-find) orange selections named 'Irish Poet'. Both are useful if planted *en masse* in borders and will bloom all summer until frost.

- Sow indoors in individual modules 4 to 6 weeks before planting.
- Keep light quality bright if growing seedlings under lights.
- Transplant emilia after all danger of frost has passed.
- Emilia may self-seed in mild climates.

BIRD'S EYE GILIA

Gilia tricolor

This native North American plant from Pacific coastal climates produces delicate stems with small purple flowers and pale-blue pollen sacks. A true, old-fashioned plant, gilia was grown in cottage gardens as long ago as the late 1700s. Gilia should be sown directly into cool soil in early spring and then lightly covered. If you own a cool greenhouse, seeds should be planted in 4-inch pots (a pinch in each) and later thinned. If sown early and kept cold yet bright, the plants can be sown much earlier (in February) and set out in late March or when the native trees like maples begin to bloom.

- Sowing seed in individual cells is possible if you are careful not to disturb the roots.

- Gilia resents being transplanted and grows best in long, cool spring weather.

- Plants stop blooming once hot, humid summer weather arrives.

VISCARIA
(GERMAN CATCHFLY)

Silene coeli-rosa

As taxonomists fiddle with the name (now *Silene coeli-rosa* but formerly *Eudianthe coeli-rosa*), viscaria is the name under which you will find this flower listed in catalogs. Long known as a classic cottage garden flower, you can quickly see why viscaria was so treasured—its color. A cool-growing annual for certain, the show will come to an end once hot, humid summer weather arrives.

- Viscaria is not the easiest to grow; be patient and prudent about temperature.

- Seeds germinate best in cold (40°F [4°C]) weather. Try growing them individually in cells on a porch or cool greenhouse in early spring.

- They are sensitive to transplanting. Carefully slip young plants into the garden in large containers near the last frost.

- Occasionally young plants are available via mail order or as a regional specialty.

VACCARIA (COW COCKLE)
Vaccaria hispanica

MEXICAN SUNFLOWER
Tithonia rotundifolia

Fast-growing cow cockles are rarely seen in gardens today, but this easy brassica grows into a baby's breath–like cloud if sown directly or carefully transplanted into borders in large numbers in early spring. Look for the white or pink varieties. They are easy to grow and, while short-lived, will brighten up dull spots in the early-summer garden. They can also be used in bouquets.

- Sow indoors early, in individual cells. Vaccaria is intolerant of transplanting.

- Another direct-sow annual, the seed can be scattered in freshly raked soil, but weed prudently and thin plants so that they are spaced 6 to 8 inches (15 to 20 cm) apart.

- Larger groups of vaccaria make a better show, creating clouds of color.

- Use twigs to help hold the plants erect.

- As soon as the summer heat arrives, the show is over. Plan on interplanting with something like Rudbeckia or snapdragon that can take over the show until frost.

Easy to grow but long overlooked, *Tithonia* holds an important position in gardening history. The large, lanky plants have stems topped off with brightly colored orange (or sometimes golden-yellow) daisy-like flowers. They look more natural in today's gardening schemes than they may have looked in Victorian days. Even more noteworthy is their ability to attract pollinators, especially butterflies, who can't resist their nectar-rich blossoms. Left to go to seed, their seedheads are relished by goldfinches and other seed eaters.

- Seeds can be started in individual pots in late spring for setting out into the garden once the weather gets warm. They can also be direct-sown in early summer when the soil has warmed.

- Quick-growing Mexican sunflower isn't fussy, other than its dislike of root disturbance.

- Mexican sunflower succeeds even in poor soil as long as it is irrigated.

- An extra boost of fertilizer though will kick-start plants to bloom like crazy by late summer.

- Plant in groups of three to five plants, set 3 feet (1 m) apart.

BLACK-EYED SUSAN
Rudbeckia spp. and hybrids

The greatest misunderstanding about the 20 or so North American–native black-eyed Susans is that they are thought to be perennial. At best, they are considered to be weak perennial. Consider all rudbeckias to be annuals, and treat them that way. Recognizable even to nongardeners, the black-eyed Susans are popular, useful, and easy to grow from seed. With many new varieties being introduced each new growing season, there are many reasons to add rudbeckia to your garden.

- Choose from many diverse species and varieties with unique colors.
- Sow seed indoors 6 to 8 weeks before the last frost date, or direct-sow outdoors once the weather warms up.
- Seeds needs light to germinate, so do not cover them.
- Grow at 60°F to 70°F (16°C to 21°C). Seedlings transplant easily. Don't pinch them back.
- Try this flower farmer trick: sow seed every 5 weeks for continual harvests.

SUNFLOWER
Helianthus spp.

Perhaps the happiest flower on Earth, the sunflower has always captivated us with its exuberance and joyful expression. They make us smile. The easiest of all flowers to grow from seed, they are often the first seed a child plants. Because they are quick to grow, they are perfect for impatient gardeners who want to see results. That said, they will still need an entire summer to mature, but at least they have size on their side, as some sunflowers can grow 12 feet tall (3.6 m) in just 2 months.

- Sunflowers need warmth to germinate. Sow outside once the weather has fully warmed up. Never start sunflowers indoors early.
- Sunflowers grow best if direct-sown. Space them carefully, as sunflowers resent being disturbed.
- Look for varieties that suit your preferences (seed production or cut flowers).
- Choose pollenless types for indoor bouquets, but consider adding pollen-rich older strains for the pollinators, as sunflowers are a primary source of the protein found in pollen for bees.

COREOPSIS

Coreopsis spp.

Current advances with the genus *Coreopsis* are astounding, and the future of this genus will change how we use them in our landscapes and gardens. With seed-raised annual species and many perennial varieties now available, if you are still planting the old 'Moonbeam' variety, you are missing out on a plant that has been transformed many times over.

The best new coreopsis will always have plant patent number on it, and that's a good thing, as it signifies that most likely your plant will be sterile, meaning more flowers. The color palette also has been dramatically improved, with bold bicolors and many pastel tones never before seen in the genus.

- Look for new varieties with a patent number at garden centers for the best performance.

- Note the mature dimensions of new varieties, as sizes vary.

- Annual varieties are easy and quick to grow from seed sown indoors under lights or in a bright, cool area like a cold frame in spring.

- Don't cover seed, as it needs light to germinate. Coreopsis transplants with little problem.

FLOWERING TOBACCO
Nicotiana spp.

Nicotiana's tubular flowers have long made them popular as garden flowers. Cigarette tobacco is also a *Nicotiana* species (*N. tabacum,* pictured left). While few home gardeners will ever roll their own cigars or make cigarettes, this is one nicotiana that is still worth growing for its stature and fragrant white or pink flowers. Most species and old hybrid nicotiana are fragrant, particularly *N. sylvestris* (pictured, bottom). Newer hybrids seem to have lost this scent.

The most useful of the nicotiana for garden designers are the green-flowered pendant species, particularly *N. langsdorffii*, with its tiny, lime-colored hanging flowers on sticky, tall, wiry stems. It will self-seed in most gardens as well.

Nicotiana seed is small, like finely ground black pepper. As such, it can be challenging to sow. Nursery-bought plants will grow fine as long as they are planted while still small with just three pairs of leaves. Rootbound plants will suffer and be a pale comparison to what they could have been. Starting your own plants is easy, and seedlings can handle careful pricking and transplanting. Seeds started in late spring will catch up to store-bought plants and perform even better.

Sow seed thinly in a seed-starting mix, but don't cover the seed—light aids with germination. Keep seed trays warm, around 75°F (24°C), and provide bright light, which is essential to keeping seedlings short and stout. As soon as the cotyledons open (15 to 20 days), lower the temperature to about 65°F (18°C) and remove seedlings from the heating mat if you are using one. Keep trays close to the brightest section of your lighting unit or in full sun.

- Allow pots to dry out completely between waterings to help control soil insects like fungus gnats.

- Set plants into the garden after all threat of frost has passed and maintain even irrigation.

DELPHINIUM

Delphinium spp. and hybrids

The very word *delphinium* evokes elegance. Delphiniums (they get their botanical Latin name from the dolphin, due to the shape of their flower) have long been desirable garden plants. Bloggers call them swoon-worthy, but many gardeners just call them unattainable. There is no getting around the fact that delphiniums are hard to grow. Yet we all try and try again, sometimes cheating and buying plants already grown and budded, but rarely will these plants attain the stature and presence that a seed-raised plant will.

At the end of the day, you may be wondering if delphiniums are worth it. The answer is yes, but that answer needs to be tempered with a good dose of reality. Delphiniums aren't growable everywhere, so be prepared to invest some time and energy to grow them right if you want to raise them well.

- Delphiniums are very much like columbine, a short-lived perennial, and often behaves more like a biennial, taking a year and a half to peak with a steady decline in the third year.

- Delphiniums adore deep, manure-enriched soil.

- Never buy a value pack of delphinium seed, and never buy seed that is simply labeled "delphinium." Look for proven, tested varieties and seed that is fresh.

- If you are buying plants, look for younger specimens and set them out early, just after frost, in a bed prepared with composted manure and compost.

- Delphiniums grow best without close neighbors.

- Strong seedlings should be hardened off outdoors in mid-spring if frost doesn't threaten. They will transplant easily but grow best if raised in individual pots.

Delphinium Varieties

Delphinium × *belladonna* strains. At 4 feet (1.2 m) tall, this variety makes a presence in the garden and is easier to grow than other hybrids. The flower stalks may be thinner and slightly less packed with florets, but the overall appearance and form are similar to the larger *D. elatum* hybrids. Most of these selections bloom on secondary stems, which are smaller but continue to show longer.

'Magic Fountains' strain. At 30 inches (76 cm) tall, this shorter strain is most popular with cutflower farmers and makes a good substitute for the much taller strains, which often are impractical if not ungrowable. Many nurseries now carry 'Magic Fountains', as do most plug growers. Their color range is nearly the same as the larger, old-fashioned Pacific strains but with half the height.

'Pacific Giant' strain. A group of tall delphiniums composed of a number of named series, such as the 'Round Table' series, which includes the familiar varieties of 'King Arthur', 'Galahad', and 'Guinevere', as well as 'Black Knight' and the 'Pacific' strain.

LARKSPUR
Consolida ambigua

Larkspurs are very much like poppies in that just as many people gush over them when they see them at farmers markets or in books. Most of us have not had much success with them in our home gardens. The difficulty with larkspurs begins with their botanical name. For a while they were considered botanically to be of the same genus as the tall, perennial, and stately delphinium. They are not.

I find larkspurs challenging, as many people do, yet there are those who will say that they are easy and carefree. They hail from the Mediterranean, and as such they act a bit more like biennials than annuals. Like fennel and many Mediterranean plants, they bloom in the early summer and set seed in late summer when it is hot and dry. The seed falls and germinates in the wetter autumn, where it grows and forms a rosette or a deeply taprooted young plant just in time for winter. They do well on the Pacific coast and in the British Isles, but not so much where winters are severe and erratic or where summers are hot and humid.

- Universally speaking, larkspurs do best when direct-sown, particularly in the autumn.

- Ideal conditions for larkspurs include full sun and deep, fertile soil that is relatively well drained and has fertilizer or manure added.

- If carefully germinated and grown bright and cool, young plants can be slipped into the garden once hardened off with little root disturbance.

- While you see larkspurs offered for sale at garden centers, steer away from them, for they will do little more than grow an inch or two taller and be disappointing. Unless you are certain that they were grown in a cold green house or cold frame, and only if they are very young plants not beginning to extend yet.

SUMMER GLOXINIA
Incarvillea sinensis

SNAPDRAGON
Antirrhinum majus

Botanically considered a perennial, *Incarvillea sinensis* is generally treated as an annual, as it comes into bloom in as soon as 10 weeks from seed. Somewhat new on the scene, the fine, ferny leaves and tubular white flowers are graceful and fresh-feeling, especially in container plantings where their midsummer color brightens up displays. Seeds germinate easily indoors under lights if started 8 to 10 weeks early, and they transplant well.

- Pinch seedlings back at least twice after the second pair of leaves.
- Best grown in containers, displays look better if you can set 8 to 10 plants per square foot, as they help hold each other up. A bit of afternoon shade helps in hotter gardens.
- Look for selections like 'Cheron White' or 'Cheron Pink'.

When choosing snapdragon varieties, look first for what you want in desired height and flower shape. Color is always a concern too, especially with mixes, as most snapdragon cultivars come in mixes that can look more like clown pants in the garden. Individual colors always seem to look good and integrate well regardless of your color palette.

Shorter growing varieties also look good in masses or when they are grown as edging on a border. For cutflowers at home, a row or two of snapdragons in the vegetable or cutting garden makes good sense as one can cut long stems without any care to the plants' appearance.

- Snapdragons look best in the garden if pinched (typically one should removed the growing point after three pairs of leaves have formed).
- Plant snapdragons densely for a good garden display.
- They enjoy cool summer temperatures and a constant drip of water into humic soil.

AFRICAN FOXGLOVE
Ceratotheca triloba

Ceratotheca triloba offers gardeners, particularly those who like to attract pollinators, a new option for high-summer blooms that delight many pollinating insects. Tall, fuzzy stalks with very foxglove-looking blossoms bloom from midsummer until frost, attracting an insane number of pollinators, including hummingbirds. *C. triloba* is not only easy to grow, but also the plants are also drought-resistant, even in poor soil.

- Sow seed indoors under lights 4 to 6 weeks before the last frost.

- Cover seed with ⅛ inch (3 mm) of soil, and water well.

- Seedlings grow effortlessly and benefit from pinching out the growing point at least once before the weather thoroughly warms.

- African foxglove often self-seeds after mild winters.

FOXGLOVE
Digitalis spp.

A true biennial, the tallest foxgloves still come from seeds of biennial selections that were started in midsummer of the previous year and set out into the garden by late summer. Newer hybrids and selections have come to fruition, blooming in a single growing season if started early enough. While these are tempting, few rival the display and grandeur of the biennial forms.

Sow foxglove seed thinly in midsummer in seed trays or even in a row in your vegetable garden. Seedlings will be small, but they transplant well if moved while young. Young plants grown in the vegetable garden or a dedicated raised nursery bed in summer must be transplanted to their final location garden by mid-September so they can establish a root hold by winter. The following spring, the show begins. If you are lucky, foxgloves will self-seed and scatter themselves throughout the garden.

- Sow outdoors or in seed trays in midsummer.

- Transplant young plants directly into the garden by late summer.

- Alternatively, sow seed indoors under lights. Foxglove seed needs light to germinate.

- Seedlings will handle transplanting well.

BRACHYCOME
SWAN RIVER DAISY
Brachyscome iberidifolia

How often a blue or purple daisy-like brachycome is over-looked by gardeners is somewhat surprising, for few annuals can deliver the punch of purple in almost every shade like *Brachycome iberidifolia*. This native of Australia has a long history with experienced gardeners. It was common in 19th-century greenhouses and in Victorian gardens. As a container plant, brachycome excel, especially if the weather remains cool in the summer. The show can continue well into mid- to late-summer if pots are kept cool and are exposed to afternoon shade.

- Brachycome is easily grown from seed sown indoors in late winter, 6 weeks before the last frost date.

- Keep the soil at 70°F (21°C) and avoid night temperatures cooler than 60°F (16°C).

- Surface-sow brachycome, as seed needs light to germinate.

- Pinch the plants to encourage bushy growth.

- Transplant to individual modules and plant outdoors after all danger of frost has passed.

TWEEDIA (BLUE MILKWEED)
Oxypetalum caeruleum

The blue milkweed has flowers that are about as true blue as you can get, this side of a morning glory. Once familiar to only the most nerdy of gardeners, this native of Brazil and Uruguay has been experiencing a comeback, although the color is so blue that it can be challenging to fit into a design scheme. While called milkweed, it is related only to the pollinator types, as few local pollinators seem to visit the flowers. Grow this for its blue color and the fabulous horn-shaped seedpods.

- Tweedia is easy to grow from seed sown in late February or March.

- Tweedia dislikes transplanting. Sow three seeds per pot and prick out all but one.

- The blue milkweed prefers cool-temperature nights (55°F to 60°F [13°C to 16°C]) and warmer daytime temperatures (60°F to 70°F [16°C to 21°C]).

- Pinch to encourage branching, or leave them alone for a single stem. Note this if planting out into a border. Once seedpods form, the plants stop flowering. Sow successive crops every 4 to 5 weeks for continual display.

FELICIA

Felicia amelloides, F. heterophylla

Like many South African plants, *Felicia amelloides* has long been cultivated as a winter-potted plant for cool greenhouses. Recently, named selections has begun to appear at garden centers for use in containers (where it performs best) and in gardens. Thanks to modern plant breeding, these newer selections of felicia don't form seeds, and as such are propagated vegetatively. While a bit more pricey than old seed-raised strains, they tend to have a longer blooming season. A second species, *F. heterophylla*, can be raised from seed as it is more uncommon in the trade. The color is more of a garden-friendly periwinkle purple than true blue. The only drawback is that the petals curve backward at the end of the day, but this is often overlooked by designers as the center of the flower is a darker blue and not sulfur like *F. amelloides*.

- Sow seeds 3 months before the last frost date.

- Felicia starts easily from cuttings.

- Botanically considered a subshrub, it is typically grown as a container plant as an annual.

PHACELIA (CALIFORNIA BLUEBELLS)

Phacelia campanularia

If there is one annual that has been overlooked in our gardens more than any other, it would be this blue gem of a flower: *Phacelia campanularia*. You are never going to find this native North American wildflower from California at a garden center, but it is a must-have for raising from seed at home. Thriving in cool climates, this native of dry, desert areas grows only during the rainy spring weather. Once summer weather arrives, the show will be over. Plant some next spring and enjoy your own superbloom, but have a backup plant to replace it once the show is over.

- Sow seeds individually into cell containers in late winter.

- Phacelia is quick growing; a sowing in early spring will bloom in 7 to 8 weeks.

- Phacelia is a taproot and resents transplanting, so handle roots gently when planting out.

ANNUAL MALLOW
Malope trifida

Most mallows in the hibiscus family perform exceptionally well in the garden, even if started early indoors from seed and transplanted. Yet malope is a plant that you can't outsmart unless you transplant very young plants with just two sets of leaves from 4-inch (10-cm)–deep pots where their roots have yet to reach the bottom. Sow malope seed directly into the garden and thin to leave a single plant every 12 inches (30 cm). If transplanting, be careful and transplant while very young, never disturbing the roots. Grown this way, malope will impress you with its height, dazzling you with dozens of pink, mauve, or white hibiscus-like flowers for much of the summer. They were a favorite of Claude Monet in his garden at Giverny.

- Direct-sow outdoors and thin the seedlings or start in larger pots and transplant them young.
- Malope prefers fertile, loamy soil with lots of organic matter and moisture.
- Stake malope with thin bamboo stakes as needed if plants seem unsteady.

HOLLYHOCK
Alcea rosea

Hollyhocks disappoint more than they thrill. The few gardens that can grow them well are usually found on farms with plenty of horse manure and air circulation to keep the foliage dry. A true biennial, they are easy to germinate in spring but won't be expected to bloom until the following year. Thankfully, many garden centers now offer biennial forms of hollyhocks in spring, which is the best way to avoid problems with rust. Look for rosettes of leaves growing in a 2-gallon (7.6 L) pot and not plants that have begun to bloom. The prettiest varieties remain those raised from seed and are worth seeking out if you are looking for extraordinary colors like chestnut brown or champagne and are willing to take a chance.

- Sow seed in spring and set out plants for blooming the following summer.
- Hollyhock grows best in climates with cool summer weather.
- Isolate plants from other hollyhocks or plant them in a separate bed dedicated to just hollyhock for a season or two to avoid or delay inevitable rust disease.
- Provide plenty of manure or compost to keep the plants healthy and strong.

ANNUAL HIBISCUS
Hibiscus trionum

A long favorite of horticulturists, *Hibiscus trionum*, or Flower of the Hour, has a fanbase that reaches back in time to most of the great gardens. Understated, it's another annual you will never find at a garden center, yet they are easy to grow at home from seed, and once you have it, plants will gently self-seed here and there around the garden. Its common name hints at its only problem, as the pale, creamy flowers with blackberry-colored centers open every morning. They last only a single day and never open on overcast days.

- Sow seed in early spring, one seed each to individual cells, and cover them slightly.
- Keep warm (70°F [21°C]) until germinated, and grow at 65°F (18°C).
- Set plants out into borders in large masses, or scatter them for a more natural effect.
- Save the seed to sow again next year or to share.
- Can be invasive in mild-climate gardens.

LAVATERA (ROSE MALLOW)
Lavatera trimestris

Gardeners get very excited when they see a border with a display of lavatera in it, for few plants provide such a burst of flowers and color in midsummer. In fact, the show can last as long as 3 months. This annual overperforms, but look for named selections, as they are the most floriferous. This is a plant that is all about abundance of blooms, but don't expect this sort of show if you are careless in transplanting or if you bought seedlings that were too mature. If you start seeds at home in individual cells, you can control exactly when they are at the perfect size to set into the garden a minimum of root disturbance.

- Start seed 6 to 8 weeks early indoors by sowing individual seeds into separate cells.
- Use sterile soil and allow the pots to dry out between waterings to reduce the threat of fungus. Rotate where you plant them every year to avoid fungal breakouts.
- Stake plants with thin bamboo stakes to keep them tall and strong.

AT-A-GLANCE

SCABIOSA
(PINCUSHION FLOWER)
Scabiosa atropurpurea

TRACHELIUM
(BLUE THROATWORT)
Trachelium caeruleum

This native of South Africa was an overnight success when it first arrived in England more than 200 years ago. It was one of the first nearly black flowers collected in the wild. The species name *atropurpurea* comes from that first collection (it means black-purple), and its earliest common name "mourning widow" also hints at its mysterious color. Scabiosas are best if started at home, as they don't take well to being transplanted. Home-raised plants can be successful if you carefully sow 2 or 3 seeds per pot and remove all but one that will make it to the garden. The genus also craves alkaline soil, so add a dusting of powdered limestone to the soil if your soil is acidic.

- Sow indoors into individual cells, 6 weeks early.
- Transplant pinched seedlings to flower beds with additional lime.
- Provide thin stakes early to support the inevitable heavy flowers to come, as the stems will tumble and become irrevocably twisty.
- Frequently deadhead scabiosa to encourage continual blooming.

With a common name blue throatwort, it's no wonder that so few have heard of or grown this flower. Long favored by savvy florists and beloved by Victorian gardeners, it is in the process of being renamed blue lace flower. Trachelium is far easier to grow than its appearance may communicate. Seeds sown in late winter or very early spring transplant easily into cells, and once set out in the garden after frost, they will tower to 3 feet (1 m).

- Start seed early indoors with warmth, covering the seed lightly.
- Trachelium transplants easily into single cells.
- Plant this outside at the same time you plant tomatoes.
- Never pinch seedlings, as the largest flowers will grow on the central stem.
- Trachelium prefers alkaline soil.

FALSE QUEEN ANNE'S LACE
Ammi majus, A. visnaga

FLOWERING CARROT
Daucus carota

All ammi must be raised from seed. Nursery-bought plants will rarely grow well unless they are tiny when you buy them. As with all members of the carrot family, these taprooted plants grow best when sown directly. They hate transplanting and root disturbance. If you are very careful, seedlings can be started early indoors or outside on a porch where it is cool and bright. *Ammi majus* can be purple or white, and they produce long, bare stems with flower umbels that wave in the wind. Its close relative *A. visnaga* has fernier foliage and greenish flowers that look quite different in the garden as well.

- Refrigerate seed at 35°F to 48°F (2°C to 9°C) for 2 weeks to ensure uniform germination.
- Cover seed lightly, as it needs light to germinate.
- Grow cold (60°F [16°C]) for the stockiest seedlings, and plant outside in large groups while still small.

A close relative of *Ammi majus* and *A. visnaga*, *Daucus carota* appears different only to botanists, as most gardeners won't notice the difference. The cultivar 'Dara' is popular with cut-flower growers and those seeking to create a pollinator garden, but the tall, wavy stems are lovely and add a Victorian charm to a formal border. It was inevitable that these relatives of the common Queen Anne's lace would eventually become cut flowers, but unlike wild Queen Anne's lace, carota's umbels never close up once cut.

- Very carefully grow single seeds in single cells like the pros do, transplanting into the garden while still very young. They dislike root disturbance.
- Allow carota to self-seed around the garden. Encourage this by not using mulch. Look for seedlings in autumn or spring to tag so that they won't be mistaken for weeds.

CUPHEA

Cuphea spp.

For more than a century, *Cuphea* species have been collected and grown as conservatory plants and as container plants. Only recently has cuphea begun to find its place in our gardens. The genus is large, with more than 260 species all native to the Americas.

The diversity of floral shape and performance is broad, with some growing no taller than a foot (0.3 m) tall, and others towering to 5 or 6 feet (1.5 or 1.8 m). The species most often hybridized or selected for ornamental culture are *C. micropetala*, *C. ignea*, and *C. hyssopifolia*. Some of the more obscure species have found their floral displays to be popular, such as *C. viscosissima*, a favorite of mine with deep magenta flowers in late summer that appear on sticky stems that attract an obscene number of pollinators.

- Surface-sow cuphea indoors 6 to 8 weeks early in a warm (70°F [21°C]) area.

- Pinch plants once they form their third set of leaves to encourage branching.

- Plants transplant easily with no problems. Set them out in garden once frost danger has passed.

CERINTHE (HONEYWORT)

Cerinthe major, C. minor

I have been so guilty of ignoring this genus for years, believing that it was too hard to grow or maybe just too fussy even for my greenish thumb. I became seduced by it first in photographs and later by acquiring the young plants (which often were expensive) from a specialty grower. I only recently discovered not only how terrific the genus is in the garden but also how ridiculously easy it is to grow from seed.

Cerinthe major is not just about the flowers but also the foliage, if not the entire plant habit (pictured left). The stems curl downward gracefully, with a glow of violet near bloom time. Garden designers love that blue-gray foliage, by itself impressive, especially in large plantings.

The pure species of *C. major* has yellow flowers with a reddish-brown band on each tubular flower. The variant *C. major* var. *purpurescens* has a wildly different color palette (pictured middle). It is the king of the clan and should be sought out to grow. It mixes well with other garden color schemes.

- *C. major* does very well if started early indoors on a warm windowsill or under LED lights.

- The seed is large enough to sow by hand (pictured bottom).

- Covered slightly and kept warm, the seedlings grow well in bright light.

Cerinthe Varieties

Cerinthe major. The species type has golden-yellow flowers with a chestnut-colored band near the base of the flowers, with bluish leaves and darker blue bracts.

C. major var. *purpursecens* 'Kiwi Blue'. The best selection, with glaucus, blue bracts gradating to a darker color near the dark violet flowers, giving the illusion of a larger floral display.

C. minor. A nice species for the garden, with slender yellow flowers and a smaller habit than *C. major* selections. Easy from seed but slower to germinate than *C. major.*

TUBEROSE

Polianthes tuberosa

Long grown for the fragrance industry and in Hawaii for their use in leis, the heirloom tuberose has nevertheless become uncommon, which is a shame, as few flowers offer its scent. Grown from bulb-like tubers found in most Dutch bulb catalogs, the tubers can be lifted in the autumn before the ground freezes. The best way to grow tuberoses is to plant them in deep containers (five or per 12-inch [30-cm] pot), and bring the pots indoors if frost threatens. In warmer climates (zones 10 or higher), tuberoses can be left in the ground, which is how they will perform best, as they are more of an evergreen perennial bulb. Look for the largest bulbs you can find.

Double and single varieties are available along with many new hybrids in new colors, such as pink or yellow. I prefer the heirloom white tuberoses, in double and especially single form.

It's common for tubers purchased from bulb suppliers to not bloom for a few years until the plants have built up enough energy to form buds. Look at the size of the bulbs before buying if you can. Ginger-root-sized bulbs are best. Hot summer weather and culturing in large pots, which you can bring into a cellar or sunroom, will help alleviate any dormancy issues. Tuberoses resent being forced into dormancy.

- Tuberoses dislike being forced to go completely dormant, so keep bulbs in pots even in the winter while storing them in a cool spot.

- Look for the largest tubers you can find, as small ones will not produce a flower stem until they have matured.

- Fertility will help. Use a balanced feed higher in nitrogen to encourage more leaf growth.

MIGNONETTE
Reseda odorata

Just speaking the word *mignonette* sounds romantic, but when was the last time you saw this rarely grown annual? We know that Thomas Jefferson kept pots of *Reseda odorata* at Monticello in 1811, and gardeners in England cultivated it as far back as 1742. Most historians, however, claim that it was Napoleon who truly made *R. odorata* famous by sending seeds back to his wife, Josephine, during his Egyptian campaign. Josephine loved the smell so much that by 1799 she named the flower mignonette ("my darling one").

Surprisingly, even accomplished gardeners and horticulturists have never been able to grow mignonette well. Even today, most seed sources often substitute the easier-to-grow *R. alba*, which has no scent at all. Be prepared though; this is not a flower you grow for its appearance.

- Grow mignonette as an exercise in experiencing history through your nose.

- Start seeds in early spring indoors, germinating at 80°F (27°C) and establishing at cooler temperatures around 55°F (13°C).

- Transplant mignonette to a large pot, three to five seedlings per pot.

- Use a sterile potting mix but add ground limestone, as *Reseda* prefers an alkaline soil closer to 7.5 pH.

SCENTED VIOLET
Viola odorata

Of all the popular flowers from the 19th century, the scented violet ruled but then disappeared completely. A century and a half ago, scented violets were the first choice for New Year's bouquets, even featured on the very first Valentine's Day cards. Millions of violets were grown around the Northern Hemisphere purely for the enjoyment of their scent in bouquets.

Economically, scented violets were a profitable crop. Violet farmers often grew sweet peas and pansies as a second crop, but it was their violet houses that got the most attention because that was where the money was.

Dozens of varieties of *V. odorata* were developed, some white, double, and many shades of purple, with names that reflect the era, such as 'Baroness Rothschild' and 'The Czar'. Most have been lost today.

- The named selections of *V. odorata* are not challenging to grow, but they do thrive in cold temperatures.

- Garden soil should be augmented with fresh compost and potting soil.

- Finding plants is the hardest thing, but there are always a few nurseries that still carry some of the true named and double-flowered antique selections.

- Frequently divide plants in late spring to retain vigor.

SWEET PEA

Lathyrus odoratus

The sweet pea is a storied but mysterious plant with intense fragrance. Its color palette is unique in the plant world for its many hues that fall within the color family of couture bridesmaid gowns, with their tints of periwinkle, lavender, the absolute palest shell pink, bright watermelon, and coral cerise, just to name a few. With hundreds of varieties bred over the years, you can create vivid arrangements using just a single color family. They are currently in demand from top floral designers for use in early summer weddings.

Although the sweet pea has a long history in Europe and North America, it fell out of favor and had been nearly absent in North American gardens starting around the mid-20th century. It was considered a specialty plant with appeal only to the truly nerdy plantspeople. But in recent years, things have changed.

◄ Sweet peas come in a wide range of colors, so think about how you might arrange them. Consider growing all shades of just one color for maximum impact.

SWEET PEA HISTORY

Much has been written about the history of the sweet pea. Many of its earliest and most notable fans approached it from the standpoint of science and research. There the sweet pea played an important role, particularly in early genetic research. Gregor Mendel, the "Father of Modern Genetics," used many pea species to support his work and found the sweet pea to be perfectly designed to demonstrate principles later known as Mendelian traits. These included how color, form, height, and even fragrance work in plant breeding. The fact that the sweet peas have a flower that generally self-pollinates helped support the work. It's also why we can save our sweet pea seeds from year to year and usually find that they "come true from seed."

In the late 19th century, breeders such as Henry Eckford of Scotland crossbred sweet peas to exhibit larger blooms, ruffles, and more fragrance. These new flowers became popular with growers, prompting a sweet pea craze that lasted well into the first part of the 20th century. The new crosses became known as "Spencer" sweet peas, named after Lady Spencer, whose gardener was involved with some early breeding.

'Burnished Bronze'

'Carlotta'

SPENCER VARIETIES

Undeniably it is the Spencer varieties that are best for cutflower use, given that most have been specially selected as exhibition varieties. These will have the longest stems, largest flowers, and the most flowers per stem, not to mention ruffles and fragrance. The seeds for these varieties are becoming more available outside of England, but it's my opinion that the finest seeds do come from the few specialty nurseries in the UK, with a couple from California. (see Resources, page 233).

While England introduced the Spencer varieties, the United States greatly improved the ones known as grandifloras or floribunda. These are more commonly sold as mixed color packets of seed by large seed companies, but single-color varieties can be found at almost any of the specialty sweet pea growers in the US and UK.

Novelty sweet peas like those with striped petals (known as flakes) or bicolored blooms where the keel is a contrasting color were once very popular Victorian types. They remain sought out by many, along with the few dwarf and semidwarf forms.

Lastly, there are some species (various *Lathyrus* species) worth trialing in pots or in the garden if you are more horticulturally curious. Very old varieties such as the original 'Cupani' and 'Painted Lady' offer small flowers in abundance, along with a stronger fragrance.

'Baronscourt'

A lavender Spencer sweet pea

HOW TO GROW SWEET PEAS

Sweet peas are cool-weather crops, although most gardeners can find the right season to squeeze some in. In the UK, seeds are often planted in the autumn or winter, indoors under glass or outside for emergence in late winter or early spring. The cool, extended springs suit sweet peas perfectly. In New England, we sow them indoors or in the greenhouse in mid-February. As cool-weather plants, seedlings can be held back by their required pinching and deep root training pots and hardened off earlier than most other annuals, sometimes as early as mid-March if the snow has melted, when they can be set into rows in the garden.

In the Pacific Northwest, San Francisco, and mild-winter areas, a fall planting lets you avoid the dry summer heat. A new market as a cut flower has expanded their range as a cutflower crop raised in hoop houses covered in plastic sheeting that can be raised and lowered to keep the crop cool. Some flower farmers can raise them as winter cut flowers, while others, such as those in northern Vermont, can have consistent harvests right through summer until fall. There are no tricks, just facts about temperature. Once hot weather arrives, the season is usually over, but in cool-summer climates, if one keeps flowers picked and seedpods from forming, a later season can be expected.

PLANTING

I recommend starting seeds indoors in most cases, but you can direct-seed in some other cases. If you do, don't be afraid to sow seed thickly, especially if you use a legume inoculant as one might with garden peas. Seeds can be sown in late autumn in the Deep South or even in the late winter or very early spring. Early spring sowings are best in the Northeast and the midwestern United States. In England and the Pacific Northwest, where sweet peas grow best, seed can be sown in the autumn, winter, or spring.

While you can choose to pinch and remove tendrils to get larger flowers, if left alone, dense plantings often look perfectly fine, except that the flower stems will be shorter and flowers smaller. The tendrils can make things messy as you try to remove stems, as they grab onto most anything nearby, especially emerging flower buds.

Sweet peas stated in deep root trainers or deep cells must be pinched as soon as the second pair of leaves form. This will encourage stronger side shoots, of which, you should leave only one or two to grow on.

The deep, straight root system of a sweet pea prefers that nothing blocks its way as it grows downward.

LEFT: White Spencer sweet peas growing on the English Cordon method.

ABOVE: A collection of Spencer sweet peas in various shades of purple and white.

Sweet peas must be grown with support, such as netting, tall canes, or a trellis structure appropriate for them. A common mistake one can make is to simply plant seedlings into the ground at the bottom of a trellis or arbor and think that the sweet peas will act like other vines like morning glories and use their tendrils to climb. They won't do so unless using brush or thin twigs. They are not a "plant it and forget about it" type of vine. You will need to tie them to stakes, canes, or netting, as those tendrils will only get in the way of plants growing tall. Once you make the first tie, the vines seem to change their mind, and within a couple of weeks, stems and leaves will begin to grow bigger as if by magic.

Space your rows far enough apart, as the rows will be tall, and shade cast from one to the next will inhibit bloom. Keeping 4 feet (1.2 m) between rows is the minimum space. As for those tendrils: while a few can be allowed to grab onto netting if using that method, you will quickly learn that tendrils will become a problem as the plants grow, so cutting them off with small scissors should become a biweekly chore. Tying stems with twine to your support system will consume the balance of your time as the plants rush skyward during June at an astonishing rate of 3 to 5 inches (8 to 13 cm) a day. Removing tendrils and keeping plants growing with just two or three stems will result in the longest-stemmed sweet peas that are straight and have significantly larger blooms.

Sweet peas grow best in a site that receives at least 6 to 8 hours of direct sunlight. They grow better planted in neat rows rather than on a typical teepee trellis. If a trellis is your only option, choose a vertical tower-type trellis like a tall tomato cage with plenty of room at the top for the flowers to expand and bloom. Late-afternoon shade, such as a cast shadow from a house or tall trees, is beneficial in hot areas.

Sweet Peas Are Not for Eating

Although they are related to garden peas *L. odoratus*, the cutflower sweet pea seeds are considered to be toxic if consumed in large quantities. Never eat the pods.

Some sweet pea varieties do well in containers. Among these are the dwarf and semidwarf strains, as well as some taller ones. Full-sized sweet peas will grow to at least 8 feet (2.4 m) tall, and they won't start blooming until they reach 5 feet (1.5 m). A large container will aid the entire process by adding weight, and one with depth will help these deep-rooted plants live longer. Care will need to be taken with watering, as once a vine dries out, foliage may yellow and buds may drop. In general, sweet peas are not ideal candidates for most containers unless you can tend to them daily.

SWEET PEA SEED

Seeds are more readily available today, even in North America, but the finest varieties will come from the few specialist growers both in the United States and England. You can save your own seed too, as most sweet peas come true to seed.

Not everyone agrees on whether you should soak sweet pea seed. I stopped soaking seed 4 years ago and find no difference in germination rates; however, bottom heat does speed up germination by about 5 to 7 days. Without heat, a tray kept at room temperature may take as long as 2 weeks to germinate. Soaking seed won't harm seeds, and many growers still insist that it works better. Soak overnight or just until the seeds begin to swell. Chipping or sanding a bit of the pea coat off of the seed is another old-fashioned but often recommended way to speed up germination.

SWEET PEAS: A FAMILY FAVORITE

I encountered sweet peas at an early age. In the 1960s, my mother kept a few bouquets of plastic flowers around the house. This seems odd to me now, for my parents were accomplished gardeners, but I can cut them some slack since it was the style back. Her plastic arrangements always keyed in on one particular specimen. It looked foreign to me because I never saw one like it in the garden. It was a single stem of pink plastic buds in an old jadeite bud vase over the kitchen sink. "It's a sweet pea," my mom told me, "but we can't grow them because they are just too difficult." That task was left to Mrs. Usher, the grandmother of the family who kept a dairy farm near us and was well known in the neighborhood for her magnificent sweet peas.

I first attempted to raise sweet peas myself around age 10. I didn't have much luck at first, but by age 20, I was entering them in midsummer flower shows held at the Worcester County Horticultural Society (now Tower Hill Botanic Garden, in Boylston, Massachusetts). One day in the mid-1980s, I brought a big basket of home-grown sweet peas to a family reunion party.

My aunt Harriett and my aunt Marion pulled me aside nearly in tears, recalling Mrs. Usher and her award-winning sweet peas, flowers they had not seen for over 50 years. Today, I still know the grandchildren of the Ushers, and I still have that same green jadeite vase. Every year I fill it with a few real pink sweet peas and remember my mother and Mrs. Usher.

The color palette of sweet peas is like no other flower, with many shades of pink, cerise, and watermelon tones, as well as periwinkle purples and lavender. On our back porch I sometimes arrange mason jars of every color.

A good deep container (3 × 5–6 inches [8 × 13–15 cm]) is required to give your sweet peas space to grow in their critical seedling stage.

As for planting containers, the deeper the better. Sweet pea seedlings produce heavy, thick, white roots that want to go straight down, which you will discover once you transplant any seedling in a deep pot. You should be able to locate deep plug cell trays. Like all legumes, sweet peas dislike root disturbance or anything getting in the way of them growing down in a pot. However, these are sturdy root systems that don't recoil at touching as some poppies or other annuals do. They prefer to be sown individually or two to three peas per pot, and should never divided be or transplanted.

The goal is to grow stocky seedlings that are properly hardened off, pinched once to promote more robust side shoots. Slide the entire rootball from its deep pot into a prepared hole in the garden in earliest spring, as soon as the weather is staying above freezing but is still cold.

▶ Feed sweet pea plants right from the beginning if you want tall plants and long stems. Don't forget amend your soil with ground limestone to the soil if your soil is known to be acidic.

FERTILIZER

Fertility is important when raising exhibition-sized flowers or the finest cut flowers. Sweet peas react positively to a weekly balanced liquid feed in the 10-10-10 range for the first month, switching to lower-nitrogen fertilizer once buds begin to form.

TROUBLESHOOTING

- Yellowing flower buds that fade and drop off are not uncommon at the beginning of the season. This is often caused by temperature differential between cold and hot nights, not by blight or fungus. Once the temperature differential moderates, stems with yellowing flower buds will stop dropping and the first flowers will open.

- Powdery mildew can be controlled by watering in the early morning to allow the foliage to dry off before nightfall.

- Once flowers begin, it is important to keep picking flowers so seedpods don't form. This shouldn't be a problem, as you will want to pick the flowers. Since their season is short in most areas and ends when hot weather arrives, deadhead any spent blooms as soon as possible.

SWEET PEA TRAINING METHODS

Sweet peas will grow to 8 or 9 feet (2.4 to 2.7 m) or even higher. This creates a training issue, since most structures and canes sold at garden centers top out at 6 feet (1.8 m) or so. Professional growers have found some ways around this problem.

Following are three methods professional growers use for staking and training sweet peas. Regardless of method, the plants should be treated basically the same. Start them indoors or outside in mild winter areas, and pinch out the main growing tip to encourage branching at the second leaf stage. When planting out, remove all but one or a few of these side shoots, and remove any additional side shoots as they emerge.

CULTURAL METHOD 1: PEA BRUSH TOWER

The best way to add sweet peas to a border or into a landscape is to provide a tall, natural, columnar trellis system for them to climb, especially if you don't want to bother with tendril removal. Such a structure looks best when sited near the back of a border, as the flowers will appear mainly at the top. Pea brush towers also do well with seeds that are direct-sown around the base of the tower in a ring.

Pea branches for use in making a brush tower can come from most any thin-yet-sturdy branching shrub or tree. I use *Fothergilla*, but birch branches also work well. Be sure to cut branches in a range of sizes from ¼ inch (6 mm) in diameter to 1 inch (2.5 cm) in diameter for strength. They must be cut the previous autumn or in midwinter, as freshly cut branches in the springtime will sprout in damp soil, and the dried sprouting growth will look messy.

Sweet peas planted out in the flower borders underneath a twig tower. These are not intended for cutting, but more as a statement in the perennial border. They will cover the brush by June and look like a tall column of color.

(continued)

CULTURAL METHOD 2:
MESH, NETTING, OR WIRE

Northern greenhouse growers use an augmented cordon method similar to method 3, but instead of bamboo canes, they simply use plastic mesh and evenly attach vines to it. I sometimes use this method with black plastic poultry netting combined with bamboo canes and end posts to reinforce the grid.

Why Cut Off Tendril's Too?

You may be wondering why sweet peas should be tied when the tendrils will happily attach to the canes if allowed to. Tendrils are the sweet peas' worst enemy. The tendrils found on the tip of each leaf become monstrously large, and each one will need to be cut off with scissors so it does not grab onto other stems. The greatest damage comes from grabbing emerging flower buds. With the tendrils removed and the stems tied to each cane, the plants will grow into steroidal giants, each one trying its best to send out more side shoots and more tendrils, all of which you will need to remove. The longest flower stems will come from those plants limited to a single stem with no side shoots. Flower stems on these cordons can be as long as 14 to 18 inches (36 to 46 cm).

Sweet peas planted out in the flower borders underneath a twig tower. These are not intended for cutting, but more as a statement in the perennial border. They will cover the brush by June and look like a tall column of color.

Removing tendrils may seem unimportant, but their removal will quickly become apparent, especially if you are growing sweet peas using the cordon method as the leaves and tendrils will be two or three times larger than sweet peas left to grow naturally. Tendrils this large will grab only new growth and will distort emerging flower buds causing crooked stems.

CULTURAL METHOD 3: CORDONS/BAMBOO CANES

The cordon method, while the most time-intensive way to grow sweet peas will get you the finest results with the longest stems and largest blossoms. It's perfect for those who like to putter and fuss in their garden after work for an hour every few days, as this method does require near constant care and attention to detail. The overall structure is very attractive with its tidy rows of neatly tied bamboo canes. They are satisfying to build and look very English.

One effective way to create the overall cordon structure is to use 8- to 10-foot (2.4- to 3-m) tall bamboo canes that are at least a half inch (1 mm) in diameter and are set in rows 6 to 8 inches (15 to 20 cm) apart. To keep the canes perfectly straight, a horizontal wire is usually pulled taut between two fence poles set on opposite ends of the row. Each cane can then be tied to this wire to be held upright. The purpose isn't just aesthetic; the goal is to train each sweet pea plant to just a single stem, which you will tie periodically to the cane. All the plant's energy thus is directed to forming flower buds and perfect blooms.

Sweet peas for the cordon method should be started early indoors in 6-inch (15-cm) deep cells. Each seedling must be pinched at the second leaf stage to slow down growth so the plants can focus on root and side branch formation. Pinching is essential in stimulating side branches. The side branches grow the thickest stems, but you only leave one side branch to eventually tie onto a cane.

Plant a single pinched seedling at the base of each cane and water in well with a bit of 10-10-10 fertilizer. Add lime if your soil is acidic. Plants may do little for a few weeks or even up to a month, but growth will accelerate as the weather warms. They will take off just after you make the first tie. Tie the long stem loosely but securely to the cane so the vine will grow upwards. Tie every 6 inches (15 cm) or so. You may need to tie every other day if the weather is warm.

Cordons of Spencer sweet peas

POPPY

Papaver spp.

Poppies are among the loveliest of all flowers. For home gardening, focus on the annual poppies—species that are either slightly biennial and sown in autumn or true hardy annuals that must be direct-sown. These include the colorful Shirley poppies (*Papaver rhoeas*), the bright red Flanders poppies, and even opium poppies (*P. somniferum*) in their many color forms. Annual poppies remain rare in gardens today despite the fact that many people want to grow them. The main reason you seldom see poppies when you walk through your neighborhood is simply that poppies are darned difficult to grow.

Growing annual poppies is like mastering watercolors: the process involves specific steps performed at just the right time, a gentle hand, and patience. Also like watercolor painting, growing poppies can become easy with attention and practice. The rewards are definitely worth it, for few flowers are as beautiful, dynamic, and special.

Annual poppies feature tissue paper-thin petals with sublime delicacy. You can tell how unique they are by some of the words used to describe them: satin, taffeta, organza, and silk. The color palette offered by annual poppies is simply voluptuous. Among Shirley poppies or breadseed poppies, you'll find an array of colors that rivals any cosmetics counter, including smoky plums, coral pinks, and even silvery grays. Iceland poppies can be found in delicious melon and fruit strains, as well as vivid colors like clown-pants yellow, fluorescent pink, and safety-vest orange. In short, there is an annual poppy for any gardener's taste or situation.

Of the nearly 100 known poppy (*Papaver*) species, only about five are commonly grown. Of these, four are considered annual (or slightly biennial), leaving the long-lived Oriental poppy as the lone, true perennial. It's a sturdy relative with blossoms as delicate as a tulip. The plants are masculine structurally and physically, with attributes like hairy leaves and stout stems that some feel minimize the impact of the fragile flowers.

◄ Clockwise from top to bottom: (1) Shirley poppy, (2) A vase of Shirley poppies, (3) Shirley poppy 'Mother of Pearl' strain introduces many smoky shades, (4) Shirley poppy, (5) Shirley poppy 'Bridal White' is an all-white strain of rhoeas the Shirley poppy that has yellow stamens, (6) Shirley poppy

OTHER SPECIES OF POPPIES

The word *poppy* is used casually to describe many cousins of the *Papaver* clan that are not true poppies. These relatives often share the cultural hurdles true poppies do, and like true poppies, they have microscopic seeds and produce seedlings that resent root disturbance.

PRICKLY POPPIES. The prickly poppies (*Argemone*) are less familiar species long valued by horticulturists. All are native to North America and must be sown by seed where they are to grow for best results. They are occasionally offered for sale by specialty seed sources, and they can be seen in gardening magazines where they are grown by knowledgeable plantspeople. A few nurseries offer well-grown young plants in larger pots, but if you want prickly poppies, you'll probably have to start them from seed. This is not an easy task. Among the challenges is the need to create a small field fire, often with pine needles sprinkled onto the surface of the soil and then ignited. The tiny surface-sown seeds germinate best if exposed to heat and smoke. If you are willing to go through all the steps, you may be astounded when you see the *Argemone*'s large, white fried egg-like poppy flowers and gorgeous prickly foliage.

Prickly poppy (*Argemone pleiacantha*)

HIMALAYAN BLUE POPPIES. Blue poppies (*Meconopsis*) can cause a near riot when they show up in conservatory or flower shows. There are at least a half-dozen true blue *Meconopsis* and still more ranging from pale yellow to violet. If you haven't guessed already, they are among the more challenging flowers within a genus that is already nearly impossible for average gardeners. So why bother discussing them? Well, I have found a work-around, albeit not a failsafe one.

Blue poppies are native to the high altitudes of the Himalayas, and they dislike heat. They are difficult but still growable if you live in a cooler area where they won't suffer in summer, such as the Pacific Northwest, New Zealand, or Scotland. My "secret" workaround is simply to look for a spot on your property that comes close to approximating these cool, moist climates and hope you get lucky. I know of three people in Vermont and one in Rhode Island who have taken a flier on blue poppies with great success. *Meconopsis*, especially the blue, are the Holy Grail of all plantspeople.

SHIRLEY POPPIES AND FLANDERS POPPIES. *P. rhoeas* is one of the most beloved of European wildflowers. One famous species, Flanders poppies, will be preserved forever in the impressionist paintings of Claude Monet and Camille Corot. Known by many as red "corn poppies," they are the model for the tissue-paper red flowers distributed around Memorial Day and Veterans Day. *P. rhoeas* can grow well in a monoculture such as a field of grain but not in denser spots or more diverse locales like a natural meadow. For best results, sow all selections of *P. rhoeas* alone, in a prepared bed where the young seedlings won't be disturbed and weeds can be kept at bay.

Red poppy strains selected over the past 200 years, known as the Shirley poppies have a peculiar yet lovely white band appearing around the edge of each petal and an extraordinary color palette that includes smoky tones of lavender, near-gray, and all shades of coral. But their beauty comes with a big caveat—they are short-lived, both as a cut flower and as a garden flower. When you see one in full bloom, however, you will wonder how any of us could live without them.

Himalayan poppy (*Meconopsis*)

Shirley poppy (*P. rhoeas*)

CALIFORNIA POPPIES. If you are looking for a less strenuous path to poppies, you can plant your own superbloom by sowing the annual California poppy (*Eschscholzia californica*). These flowers prefer dry-summer areas, such as California and the American Southwest. They can be grown almost anywhere if you sow them with care. A cleared spot along a concrete walk, a green space between the street and sidewalk, or a gravel bed that gets hot suit them well. They do not care for containers or being crowded into a mixed flower border.

You can sow California poppies by sprinkling them on the ground, but a more reliable tactic is to plant a couple of seeds in deep cell trays in early spring and set them outdoors to germinate. Once they do, carefully slip them out of their containers into holes in sunny spots in the garden. They will self-seed, but if you use mulch or are too aggressive in raking out the garden in spring, the tiny seedlings may never take off.

Today there are plenty of colors and varieties of California poppies to choose from, including fancier hybrids, crosses with ruffled petals, and a broader color palette with shades of pale yellow through pink.

BREADSEED POPPIES. Among all of the annual poppy species, the opium or breadseed poppies (*P. somniferum*) are perhaps the most growable. The seed is slightly larger than other poppies (you can actually see it with the naked eye), which allows you to sow seed more broadly. They share the same cultural needs of all the other annual poppies. Self-seeded "volunteers" are probable, more vigorous, and easily identifiable than slower developing plants like Shirley poppies.

Like all poppies, they enjoy an open site and rich, well-drained soil. You can raise them to a large, bold statement flower as long as you approach them confidently and thin them to a plant every 10 inches (25 cm) or so.

P. somniferum is manageable and even satisfying in a home garden as the seed germinates readily and often profusely. They come in many strains and varieties, ranging from puffy pompom types to fringed selections. In color, they range from deep, plummy tones to red and white bicolored flowers, such as the variety known as Danish Flag. Like all poppies, they naturally have four petals, but doubles have eight, and pompoms have plenty more.

California poppy (*Eschscholzia californica*)

The Legal Status of Poppies

Opium poppies (*P. somniferum*) contain opiate alkaloids that are the active ingredients in many narcotic drugs, legal and otherwise. They are contained in the latex of the seedpod. So is it legal to grow them? The answer is yes and no. Many reputable seed catalogers and nurseries offer them in both seed and seedling form, most often the breadseed variety or non-opium ornamental strains. Nevertheless, the USDA does classify these poppies and their derivatives as controlled substances. The *P. somniferum* plant produces blooms of unrivaled beauty and uniqueness that many gardeners cherish as ornamental plants. But if you are uneasy about the legality, there are plenty of other beautiful poppy varieties you can grow without fear.

▶ Opium (breadseed) poppy (*P. somniferum*)

ICELAND POPPIES. Botanically considered a biennial, most gardeners treat these beautiful poppies as an annual because they do well in pots. Often sown in early spring or in late winter for cool-garden planting, the Iceland poppy (*P. nudicaule*) is best if treated as a temporary display plant in your garden. They are wonderful in spring mixed containers. As a cut flower, the Iceland poppy excels, which is why it is the most common poppy among cutflower farmers. It is best if picked while still in bud, just when the two calyxes begin to split like a walnut and the color of the petals can be seen within. To stop the latex from weeping, the cut stem end can be dipped into scalding water ever so briefly or burned over a candle for just a second. This applies to all poppies, but if you bring a bud vase into the garden with you, it is unnecessary.

The Iceland poppy is the easier-to-grow sister of the Shirley poppy. Most garden centers carry them in the spring along with pansies and other cold-tolerant plants, and its flowers are just as graceful as any poppy, if not prettier. Raising Iceland poppies from seed takes more skill and is difficult for most people.

Poppy plugs can be purchased from wholesalers who sell primarily to the cutflower trade, or you can buy plants in bud and use them in spring containers for a temporary display. Iceland poppies have some fantastic color strains, ranging from pastel mixes of pale pink and apricot to harsher clown-pants colors.

◀ There are many seed strains of *P. somniferum* and most are variable. Double or feathered strains wil typically also present some single flowers, but when one sees a truly double coral peony-type like this one, hope rises that the entire seed packet might deliever a high percentage of double blooms.

▲ Iceland poppy (*P. nudicaule*)

HOW TO DIRECT-SOW POPPIES

1. As soon as the ground thaws, rake out the area where you intend to sow seed.
2. Prepare your tools and materials.
3. Mix about a ½ cup of dry sand with a packet or two of poppy seeds. Combine the sand and seed together in a bowl.
4. Put the sand/seed mixture into a sieve and sift it evenly and thinly over the planting area.
5. Tamp down the soil with a brick or a board to set the seed into the surface of the ground—it needs light to germinate. Mist with water.
6. After 20 days or so, look for tiny seedlings. Learn to differentiate weeds from poppy seedlings. Thin the seedlings gently, leaving one seedling per 4 inches (10 cm). Keep an eye on watering, as dry spells can occur even in spring.
7. By early June, poppy seedlings will begin to look like arugula, and depending on the variety, they may begin to form flower buds. Stake plants with twine and canes or dried pea brush.
8. As poppies begin to bloom, pick them daily and remove spent blossoms and seedpods of colors that you don't want to save. Poppies will decline rapidly once summer takes hold and the temperatures rise. It isn't uncommon for seedpods to abort or decay in humid areas before they are fully mature.

You'll Need:

- Fine, sifted sand the texture of sugar (sift it first to remove any clumps)
- Kitchen sieve
- Poppy seed
- Surface protection, such as poultry netting and landscape stakes

Papaver somniferum, or bread seed poppy, seed pods should be left to mature in the garden even though they add value to flower arrangements while still green. Always leave a few until they dry and become brittle as this is how seeds for next year's plants will sow around your garden naturally.

HOW TO START POPPIES IN TRAYS

If you have a greenhouse or are home during the day in early spring to move seed trays frequently, you have a good option for raising annual poppies. They can be raised from seed using deep cell trays or root trainer pots as long as you can provide bright light and cold temperatures. The hardest part for me is culling all but one seedling from each cell, but it must be done to get full-sized plants.

Sowing tiny poppy seed can be tricky. It helps if you have a handheld seeder (the kind you tap with your finger), or you can try to sprinkle just a small number on the surface of a plug tray that has been filled with a professional potting mix. Kept cold in a cold frame, bright garage window, or even on a deck, seeds should begin to sprout. Move them indoors if hard a frost occurs. Even in a greenhouse, spring sunshine can get too hot, so all of my poppy plug flats go outdoors on days above freezing starting in mid-March.

Starting poppies in cell trays is a doable method that works for many hard-to-find annuals, even those that dislike transplanting. If kept in full sun for part of the day and exposed to wind and the weather, seedlings can be poked out of their cells (with a pencil from below, never by pulling) by the time they form their first true leaves. One trick for getting plugs out of their trays is to allow the soil to dry out so the soil separates from the container walls, keeping the root mass intact.

Plant close together—poppies look best with their brothers and sisters nearby to lean on. Keep other plants at a distance to allow good air circulation. Once planted, water the poppies in well and keep them weeded.

These *P. rhoeas*—the self-sowing 'Flanders Poppies' once bloomed—across France and Belgium seeding as a weed in wheat fields, but they are less common today with the advent of herbicides. A parent of the Shirley poppy, they are still valued in our gardens.

FERTILITY

Naturally high feeders, poppies bloom best when fed a diet low in nitrogen. A tomato fertilizer (2-10-10) or something of similar makeup will do nicely. Too much nitrogen encourages foliage to grow faster and causes soft stems that can break in the wind. If you're using a granular or dry fertilizer, including manure or organic powders, add it to the soil before planting. Liquid feed may be added at any time and is easier to apply.

LILY

Lilium spp.

There are so many flowers with common names that include "lily" that it can be confusing. Of course, it doesn't matter to florists or those buying flowers for arrangements if a calla lily is a true lily or if an Easter lily is hardy or not. But while anyone may call a black-spotted orange lily a tiger lily, gardeners who want to succeed need to know that there are a number of spotted lily–like flowers commonly referred to as tiger lilies, but there is only one true tiger lily (*Lilium lancifolium*). For the purposes of this chapter, a true lily is any plant within the genus *Lilium* and, more specifically, one that grows from a scaled bulb (a typical feature shared among all lilies).

Lilies are some of the easiest flowers to grow and most rewarding of all garden plants due to their long life in gardens with soil rich in organic matter, adequate moisture that drains well, and at least half a day of direct sun. Lilies don't ask for much but setting them up for success will help them stay with you longer. Even a lily bulb from the bargain basket at a drugstore may bloom and grow and even become the star of the garden. They are often long-lived in raised beds, berms,

rock gardens, and stone wall-lined beds where the soil is well irrigated so roots rarely sit in water. When grouped in flower borders, they can reach up far above neighboring plants to show off their often-fragrant flowers.

Compared to other perennials, lilies are often inexpensive as well, so a raised bed in the vegetable garden dedicated to just lilies makes complete sense, particularly for those who love cut flowers. Even though few of us seem to think of summer garden lilies as cut flowers, they are perfect candidates and look stunning in a tall vase.

Lilies can thrive in containers, although by autumn, they should be replanted into the garden. I often first grow lilies in containers the first year if the bulbs arrive extra large. Containers allow you to grow plants away from foot traffic, and once buds appear, they can be positioned near a doorway, on steps, on a stone wall, or on a terrace. The more the merrier when it comes to planting potted lilies. The best displays have six or more bulbs, but a large single bulb can be just as effective in a heavy pot.

◀ I could never imagine July without the creamy, tooth paste-like scent of trumpet lilies.

TYPES OF LILIES/LILY DIVISIONS

There are many types of lilies, including hundreds of named varieties and species, as well as newer interspecific crosses. Lily growers have classified all lilies into groups or categories based on their various traits. Each group, or division, includes lilies that share something in common with one another, usually based on where the original species originated from. While there is a division specifically for wild species, most gardeners grow complex crosses, often created by crossbreeding three or more species.

DIVISION 1: ASIATIC HYBRIDS

Most common in our gardens, Asiatic lilies come from crosses made with Chinese species. There are more Asiatic hybrids than with any other lily division. The group is subdivided into other groups based on their flower shape (downfacing, upfacing, outfacing, and so on) and includes some of the most familiar of lily species such as *L. lancifolium* (syn. *L. tigrinum*), the common tiger lily.

DIVISION 2: MARTAGON HYBRIDS

Martagon lilies are some of the most choice and often the most costly of all lilies. Mainly crosses of European species, many from high-elevation climates, the martagons all share a love for cool northern woodland gardens, have a pendant and waxy turk's cap-like flowers, and produce stems with attractive, whorled leaves.

▸ Martagon lilies seem to come and go in the trade, usually uncommon. They enjoy cooler summer temperatures. Their whorled foliage and thick, waxy turk's cap flowers appeal to lilly enthusiasts as well as to garden designers. A colony of them adds tremendous horticultural value to the garden.

Outfacing Asiatic 'Istanbul'

DIVISION 3: CANDIDUM HYBRIDS

This division, while more uncommon in the trade, includes hybrids created from *L. candidum* (the Madonna lily), which was once quite popular in the mid-20th century but rarely offered today. It is worth seeking out. Division 3 consists strictly of lily crosses between the species *L. candidum* and a handful of rarely found species, many of which are native to Europe.

DIVISION 4: AMERICAN HYBRIDS

This division includes many crosses made from species native to North America. These are all choice and hard-to-find lilies, but they are worth seeking out if you have the cool, woodland conditions that they love. Most are turk's cap or hanging pendant types with plenty of spotting and include *L. canadense* and *L. superbum*.

DIVISION 5: LONGIFLORUM HYBRIDS

Most people are familiar with the white Easter lily. This division includes most white trumpet lilies such as *L. longiflorum* and *L. formosanum*.

Sometimes I order so many lilies that nurseries send me some to try. These pink Easter Lilies that are taller than I am.

DIVISION 6: TRUMPET AND AURELIAN HYBRIDS

Big, fragrant, and waxy trumpet lilies are perhaps the most stately and elegant of garden lilies. Once very common, the plants are not seen in many flower gardens, as nurseries rarely carry them while in bloom. These are some of the finest of lilies, from the regal type with dark burgundy staining on the outside of the petals to the many tall hybrids in golden-yellow, orange, chartreuse pink, and apricot colors. Aurelian lilies have wider trumpets and are the result of crossing two different hybrid lily divisions (like Oriental lilies and trumpet lilies). Becoming more popular with gardeners, these are often some of the most outstanding lilies for gardens as they are taller, with larger flowers and more resistance to diseases. The odd name "Aurelian" comes from the French village of Orléans, where these outfacing trumpet hybrids were originally bred. Most trumpet lilies have pendant flowers, however, and come from a complex mix of western Chinese, Burmese, and Himalayan species such as *L. regale*, *L. sulphureum*, and *L. leucanthum*.

DIVISION 7: ORIENTAL HYBRIDS

Some of the most spectacular of lilies are found in the Oriental hybrid division. Most come from complex crosses of primarily Japanese species, such as *L. auratum* (the gold band lily) and *L. speciosum*. Most people are familiar with 'Casa Blanca' and 'Stargazer', but there are plenty of newer and, I think, much nicer crosses available from lily growers.

'African Queen' and 'Copper King' are now seed-raised strains, as the original clones of these two orange trumpet lilies developed by the late Jan de Graaf have been lost. Great variability exists, especially in color and vigor. These 'Copper King' selections are some of the first available again as growers attempt to increase stock of strains.

'Black Dragon' trumpet lilies

DIVISION 8: INTERDIVISIONAL HYBRIDS

The new lilies on the block are crosses between other divisions, such as those between the Oriental lilies and the trumpets often sold as Orient Pets. These are spectacular newcomers are surely worth adding to your garden. Most have larger flowers and stronger stems. Some are marketed as "tree lilies," and most are extremely beautiful. Oriental/trumpet crosses are properly referred to as OT hybrids, while *L. longiflorum*/Asiatic crosses are known as LA hybrids. OA hybrids are derived from Oriental/Asiatic crosses. Even more complex acronyms are being introduced as each of these interdivisional crosses is being crossed with each other.

DIVISION 9: SPECIES LILIES

Pure species, be they from Asia, North America, or Europe, are included in this division. Most are valued additions to gardens, but one should be familiar with their needs, as most are challenging to grow.

Orient or Intersectional Lilies are new and sensational. Many seem to be more resistant to the Scarlet Lily Beetle and produce larger flowers on taller stems.

Complex crosses between two different lily divisions are often the strongest stemmed, most robust growing, and most disease resistant of garden lilies.

PLANTING LILIES

Setting aside the challenges of a couple of divisions and the pure species, hybrid Lilies are some of the easiest flowers for new gardeners to grow, no more difficult than tulips. Like most bulbs, they form their flower buds a year in advance or by the previous autumn, so when you receive a bulb, it most likely will produce some flowers during the first year.

Lily bulbs are best if ordered from specialty nurseries in the summer for late fall delivery. Fall planting is the best way to ensure that you will get first dibs on many of the very special varieties offered by the handful of lily nurseries. The bulbs are healthier and most will still have active roots, and there is less of a chance of internal buds being harmed by poor storage over winter.

If you don't care about variety or would rather wait until spring, there are plenty of older commercial varieties that are propagated and distributed through the Netherlands. These include many fine lilies such as 'Casa Blanca' and other Asiatic and Oriental lilies. These can be found in spring bulb catalogs, at garden centers and nurseries in plastic bags, and sometimes in pots. Always check to see if the bulbs are sprouting, and if so, choose the ones with the least amount of growth as ideally they should still be dormant.

Trumpet lily bulb being planted in November.

▲ Lilies look best planted in large groups, something few gardeners seem to do. Ten bulbs can cost as much as a hydrangea but be even more impressive when they bloom.
▶ Down-facing Asiatic lilies like these 'Ariadne' are as graceful as Japanese lanterns in the garden.

STOCK

Matthiola incana

Stock has seen limited sowing in home gardens because it is seldom available at garden centers or nurseries as transplants in spring. More commonly, it is found at florists as a cut flower only. But fragrant stock is slowly coming back into our lives, as it has become more common to find stock sold for early spring container displays. While these 6- or 8-inch (15- to 20-cm) group pots look lovely for use in early seasonal displays, they hardly could be considered cut flower worthy and are too mature for planting out in the border. Also, the varieties selected and how they were treated (usually with hormones to make them bloom early while still in pots) will negatively affect how they perform in the garden.

Stock is a flower that should never be planted when in bloom or even when showing flower buds. If you are lucky enough to live near a small nursery that raises their seedlings for experienced gardeners, look there for stock seedlings that are still small, in individual cells, and with fewer than three sets of leaves. For most of us, however, the best results will come from raising our stock from seed in late winter or very early spring. If you are looking for long-stemmed cutflower stock, seek varieties specially bred for height and bloom quality. You likely will have to start them at home yourself.

Stock seedlings can be set outdoors on warm days in early spring to gradually harden-off if temperatures are above freezing.

◂ Stock flowers

THE STOCK STORY

Botanically, stock is a brassica (in the cabbage family). If you look closely, you can see it in their cross-shaped, four-petaled flowers. Many consider it to be one of the oldest of cottage garden flowers, with records of it being considered an "antique" if used in gardens going as far back as 300 years ago.

Early 20th-century seed catalogs often had pages of different stock varieties ranging from winter-blooming strains for greenhouse crops to shorter bedding varieties and those best for cut flowers in the garden. Most floral guides recommended it for filling gaps between daffodils and summer annuals, which hints at stocks' love of cool weather. Some stock varieties were commonly grown as annuals, particularly in England, where a July sowing could be winter-covered in a cold frame and then set out. Able to withstand light frosts, stock should be as widely used as pansies, but perhaps it suffers from not being all that marketable when not in bloom.

VARIETIES

"Stock" may strike you as a strange name for a flower. Most botanical historians believe that the name comes from an old way of referencing a stick or a trunk, referring to the often-woody base of the plant, like the sturdy stem of a cabbage, which was unique among most quick-growing cottage flowers. The names of old varieties come with an even longer list of old-timey names, most of which relate more to how the plant looks or where stock has been most popular—usually England, the epicenter of stock enthusiasm. Some older books may suggest hoary stock (a particularly gray-leaved variety), Brompton stock or ten-week stock. All are very old names of selections known collectively as summer-blooming stock in England, although they should be grown as a spring crop in most other areas.

Commercially, there are an immense number of stock varieties or cultivars, most of which can be organized by the use they were bred for. Field stock or greenhouse stock are long-stemmed cutflower varieties, many of which are fine in borders or a cottage garden. But because of their height, they may require close planting or staking to hold stems erect. Bedding plant and potted plant varieties exist too but are often difficult to distinguish simply by the variety name. Always look at the grow sheets or cultivation guides to find the perfect height and bloom style you want.

As with most brassica crops, choosing the newest stock varieties will help get you the most exceptional results. Great progress comes with science, and while old varieties may look lovely in the garden, they are more likely to be susceptible to disease or pathogens in the soil, and they are also more likely to produce only single flowers rather than the preferred doubles.

WHERE AND WHEN TO GROW STOCK

Stock is a classic cool-weather crop that will fail where summers are hot and humid. It can be raised in many plant hardiness zones, however, as long as it is started early indoors and set out just as the frost risk lifts in earliest spring. It thrives and does best where springtime is long and cool, and it does even better where summer is also long and cool. For most gardeners, though, it makes more sense to raise stock strictly for spring bouquets. Once flowering is

Some Common Stock Varieties

- Stock (*Matthiola incana*)
- Harmony
- Cheerful (good for field, bedding, and greenhouse)
- Avalanche
- QIS Series
- Lucinda Series
- Glory Series
- Iron Series
- Katz Series (tall and good both for cut flowers and the garden)
- Night Blooming Stock (*Matthiola longipetala*)

over in early summer, set out secondary fast-growing crops like zinnia or aster (*Callistephanus*).

In most gardens, stock is strictly a seasonal plant. It is an excellent addition to planting lists in mild-winter climates where temperatures rarely drop below freezing or as a late winter/early spring bedding plant in more moderate zones. Once the summer heat arrives, the plants should be near the end of their bloom period anyway, and something else can be planted.

GROWING STOCK

If you find stock already in bud or bloom, it is too late to plant into the garden unless you are looking for a 2-week-long temporary display. Stock that is already in bloom is fine for spring containers, where you can combine nursery-grown plants with spring bulbs and pansies. All will last about as long as a pot of daffodils will last in bloom. For use elsewhere in the garden, look for the smallest plants you can find. Younger is infinitely better than plants that are already beginning to extend their stems. Ideally no stem showing with three pairs of leaves is the best size to set out in the garden.

If acclimated to cold weather for a week, stock can tolerate and even prefers nippy nights and cold, breezy early spring weather. Fertile, well-drained, but moisture-retentive soil is best, much like you'd find in a raised bed in the vegetable garden. Remember that it's a brassica, and as such it enjoys the same conditions that other fast-growing brassicas like mustard and radishes enjoy.

Stock is a short-season crop, so if the weather becomes hot and humid earlier than usual, it may bloom earlier and not reach its full potential. If temperatures rise too quickly and stay above 60°F (16°C), the plants may not set flower buds at all. Early in, early out is the trick when it comes to growing stock. Sowing seed directly into the garden works well for those in cool summer areas, but in zones 5 and higher, you risk running into hot weather before flower initiation starts. The ideal range for stock to perform well, in a greenhouse or outdoors, is between 50°F and 60°F (10°C to 16°C).

Stock flourishes when planted in rows in the vegetable garden, where you can cut it for arrangements and not

The spicy-scented Matthiola in cana or 'stock' remains a popular cut flower among flower farmers.

worry about how the plants will look afterward. In fact most cutflower varieties, if not pinched, produce one long stem, and once picked, the plant could be removed for the season. If growing stock as a border plant or in containers, a pinch will help extend the bloom period. Simply pinch out the terminal growing point just as the plant begins to form a stem.

Like cabbage or broccoli, stock will grow to its most exceptional self if provided with average vegetable garden soil and moderate fertility, as overfeeding can cause weak growth. Stock grows best with fertilizer treatments that are lower in nitrogen and higher in potassium. High nitrogen will cause soft growth and yellowing leaves from the bottom, while low potassium is more critical, causing bud yellowing and leaves that will yellow starting at the tip. A good source of potassium (the *K* in N-P-K fertilizer mixes) is potassium nitrate, which is the quickest to activate. You can also treat your soil with wood ash (the potassium is released slowly) the preceding autumn.

Taller cutflower varieties may need staking, but if set into the ground close together, they are more likely to hold each other up. Pinching is the alternative if you can accept shorter stems but bushier flowering plants.

PEONY

Paeonia spp.

Peonies are beloved by many people, and it's no wonder. Few flowers offer as many benefits as peonies: ease of culture, fragrance, impressive displays, and longevity, to name a few. However, peonies can't be grown anywhere, as they are primarily northern plants that perform best in areas with long, cold winters and humid summers. Technically a woody perennial, the 30 or so peony species are mostly Asian, but a couple are native to western North America and a few are European.

The most common peony is *Paeonia lactiflora* and its many hybrids. They feature fragrant, blousy blooms in almost every shade of white, pink, and maroon, with hundreds of named crosses. Species of peonies from Asia and Europe are becoming more popular with plant collectors and adventurous gardeners. The flowering perennial most people visualize when imagining a peony are the Asian species (*P. lactiflora*) and its many crosses.

The first peonies arrived in the West from Asia in the mid-19th century. They are useful both as landscape plants and as cut flowers. Arguably as romantic as a rose, the peony has recently experienced a boom in popularity, reversing a few decades of disinterest. They are very popular these days at weddings, as the peony season is smack in the middle of June for most gardeners.

◂ A large bed dedicated to just peonies (like this one in Woodstock, Vermont) makes care and maintenance easier to manage. Widely spaced rows allow for easy weeding and picking, and aside from a fresh blanket of compost every year, the plants enjoy a wide root run and good air circulation with no competition from neighboring plants.

Many of the peonies in my current garden were transplanted from neighboring farms by my grandmother way back in the 1920s, and these are still going strong.

Peonies are grouped by type. First, there are the herbaceous peonies that die back to the ground every winter. Second, there are woodier "tree peonies," which are not really trees but small shrubs or woody-stemmed perennials. Another group is the newer Itoh hybrid, or the "intersectional" peonies that are a cross between the herbaceous and the tree types. The last group, unfamiliar to most home gardeners are the many wild species of peonies available from specialty nurseries, many of which are sought by collectors and make magnificent garden specimens. Species like *P. veitchii*, *P. rockii*, *P. obovate*, and the famed 'Molly the Witch' (*P. daurica* subsp. *Mlokosewitschii*) are always the first to go at botanic garden rare plant auctions.

Peonies are longest-lived in zones 3 to 8, as they do require a long winter's rest. They also do best if planted away from other plants, especially shrubs and trees. As such, most serious peony growers set peonies out in rows in a garden dedicated to just peonies or in a cutting garden. While you can certainly set plants out in a perennial border, remember to keep other plants at a distance, as each plant will produce roots and foliage rivaling that of a large hydrangea once they mature. It is easy to underestimate the eventual mature size of a peony, especially the Itoh hybrids, which make spectacular mounds of foliage.

Appreciative of fertile soil and good drainage, peonies also need a lot of water, so choose a site that is not unlike a vegetable garden plot: fertile soil and irrigated but never soggy. Some elevation helps, such as in a raised bed along an elevated wall garden or hillside, as this is often where they grow in the wild.

THE PEONY IN ASIA

The peony is culturally valued in much of Asia, particularly in China and Japan. Many of us forget that it is a relatively new arrival to Western gardens (within the last 150 years). It is the Chinese and Japanese who have genuinely embraced the peony as far back as Confucius in 551 BCE. Peonies in China may have been one of the first cultivated flowers, and hundreds of ornamental varieties were developed over the centuries. During the Tang dynasty (7th century), the peony became highly cultivated and treasured, and today throughout China, the peony is highly valued both medicinally and in artwork.

In Japan, peonies are even forced in late winter, grown in soil that is heated with coals or steam and protected from late snowfall with elaborate straw "hats" suspended overhead. The famous Snow Peony festival in Ueno Park every February has been a favorite stop for me in Japan. Peonies in full bloom with snow all around them is a sight I will never forget.

FLOWER TYPES

Peonies have many flower types, from single-flowered blooms with a big boss of yellow stamens to semidoubles and doubles. Flowers that have a row of single petals around a dense pompom in the center are known as a "bomb" by peony growers. There are also many novelties, ranging from mutated ones with twisted, thin petals to those with entirely green flowers.

As for garden varieties, there are many that are excellent cut flowers but only a few that are considered useful landscape plants. The latter should be sought out by those looking for an upright, sturdy plant that you don't need to stake. As anyone who grows peonies knows, staking is a big project needed every spring. It is necessary for most peonies though, and while one can buy premade wire peony rings, a suitable and often more attractive method is to construct a box-like cage with four bamboo canes set into the soil around a plant, with four horizontal canes tied in a square just under the blooms.

Peony color is affected by both soil and light, so take notes on each variety that you grow, focusing on the color of the bud when you picked it versus the color the petals displayed when opened. Regional differences are commonly based upon soil chemistry. A variety like 'Coral Charm' can have a brilliant coral color when it first opens, but indoors it will fade to a buff color.

Peony 'Coral Charm' is charming indeed by color changing from bright coral to peachy-buff as it ages. Popular with flower farmers and floral designers, it can also be grown in your garden.

ITOH HYBRIDS

In Japan, the peony has always been popular and highly treasured. In 1948, Toichi Itoh, a horticulturist from Tokyo, crossed the yellow tree peony 'Alice Harding' to the herbaceous *P. lactiflora* 'Katoden', creating a brand-new category of peonies called the intersectional peonies or, colloquially, the Itoh hybrids. Today these are known as exceptional landscape and flowering plants and are highly recommended for their lovely flowers (which come in many yellow tints) but even more so for their foliage and habit, which rivals that of any other seasonal shrub for visual appeal through the summer. Itoh peonies die back to the ground every autumn. Slower growing, which is often reflected in their high cost, the Itoh hybrids are perhaps the most beautiful garden peonies you can add to your garden.

Itoh Peony 'Bartzella'

Itoh Peony 'Misaka'

SOIL PREPARATION

Planting peonies can be tricky, as there is a right way and many incorrect ways. You may be accustomed to simply digging a hole in the garden and sliding in a rootball. But when planting peonies, a few extra steps are helpful, if not essential. Since peonies are long-lived, you should amend the site with bone meal and slow-release fertilizer that will last a few years and also get new plants off to a good start. The guidelines for planting peonies are very much like that of planting other long-lived perennial crops such as asparagus and rhubarb, which also dislike disturbance once planted out.

Old soil-prep methods may sound old fashioned, but honestly, advice hasn't changed much for 150 years. The absolutely perfect way to prep peony soil advocated in 1910 still holds today, but since it is harder to find fresh stable manure to line our 2-foot (61-cm)–deep trenches, a few adjustments need to be made. Remember, this is a plant that can and will live in this spot for dozens of decades.

Soil pH is also a good thing to adjust before planting. Even though peonies are tolerant of acidic soils, they prefer a higher pH in the 7.0 range, which is alkaline. The addition of ground limestone is a smart idea when planting a new bed and as an annual application done once in the autumn—scratch in a cup of limestone in a 2-foot (61-cm)–wide circle around each plant in the fall.

You can buy composted manure at most garden centers, and a layer is still recommended for the bottom of that 2-foot (61-cm) hole you are digging. You can also add organic slow-release fertilizer (a balanced formula) or an inorganic slow-release feed. Another layer of soil will protect the tender spring roots, leaving you a hole that is about the same depth as your pot.

Fertilizing peonies in early spring

Herbaceous peony emerging in early spring.

Ants on a peony bud are a very common sight in spring. They do no harm.

ANTS

Ants love peony buds. They are there not to help open the buds, as many myths claim. They are only there for a little snack on the sweet, sugary substance excreted by the buds. They do not harm the flowers.

PLANTING PEONIES

Peonies are unique in the plant world because they act much like perennials in the garden to our eyes, but botanically they are in fact a bit more like lily bulbs crossed with a shrub. Like lilies, they should never be moved in the early spring or before they have bloomed, and they form their flower buds a year in advance. Those dormant, pink nubs that appear on the roots in the fall are next season's growth buds that have already been established by late summer the previous season. Peonies are very specific about how deep they are planted. Too deep and they will suffer. Too shallow and winter damage can cause problems. The ideal planting depth has the crown of the bulb 1 to 2 inches (2.5 to 5 cm) below the ground.

DISBUDDING

Most peony cultivars produce several buds, but it is highly recommended to snap off all but one flower bud while they are still small. Disbudding will create the most beautiful flowers by focusing all the plant's energy on producing just one flower per stem. If you prefer, leaving two or even three buds is okay, but any more could cause the primary bud to abort, or the smaller buds may never open. If the buds do not open, in some varieties, the large central dead blossom leaves an unsightly scar.

WATERING

Peonies dislike overly mucky or wet soil, but they do appreciate plenty of water as long as the soil is well draining. Water is essential, especially in the spring when the flowering stems are emerging and the buds are maturing. It is also critical just after the blooms fade, which perhaps is the most critical time to water. Early spring rains are frequent, but by late June and July, many areas heat up, and droughts can occur. This first summer drought period around July 1 is something to monitor, as this is when peony plants are already forming their buds for next year. By late July and August, however, droughts have little adverse effect on plants.

PICKING AND STORING PEONY FLOWERS

Peonies make sensational cut flowers, but most people don't know about their ability to last in cold storage for months at a time if picked at the right stage. Cut the stems when the buds are still round like a ping-pong ball but soft like a marshmallow. Wrap the stems in dry newspaper and refrigerate for up to 2 weeks. If stems are set into the water and the buds are slightly firmer, flowers can be held back for as long as a few months.

Picked peonies bring drama and beauty to any room.

FALL CLEANUP

A lot of recent thinking about fall garden cleanup points to its harmful effects on overwintering beneficial pollinators, which is a valid and important point. But when it comes to many ornamental plants, particularly herbaceous peonies and irises, the removal of dead foliage and stems is highly recommended, as far more damaging diseases are encouraged with dead plant material. Herbaceous peonies should have all of their foliage and stems removed. Cut off 1 inch (2.5 cm) or so from the base after the first hard frost to ensure that fungus diseases and harmful insects overwintering will be reduced. Use a sharp knife or secateurs rather than a hoe or pulling the stems off, as this can damage new buds just below the surface.

WINTER CARE

While herbaceous peonies are completely cold hardy, damage from frost heave during the first winter is about all you need to worry about. A thin layer of mulch will help in this case. Tree peonies, however, are more sensitive to irregular winter temperatures, performing best in mild winter areas such as zones 6 and higher. With tree peonies, the buds are already formed. They are not underground but form on the ends of woody stems. Straw mulch within a snow fence is sometimes used in the far north to protect these buds, while a thick layer of wood mulch or leaves at the crown can add an extra layer of insurance. Both must be removed immediately at the first sign of spring.

LAVENDER

Lavandula spp.

Lavender is a highly desirable garden plant that is surrounded by myths and misinformation. It's true that lavender can be challenging to grow, especially if you live in an area that has plenty of summer rainfall combined with heat and humidity, followed by long, wet winters. If you've killed more lavender than any other garden plant, you are not alone.

Gardeners from California, Colorado and the mountain states, or anyone who enjoys a Mediterranean climate may be thinking, "What's all the fuss about lavender? It grows like a weed for us!" Perhaps, but getting lavender to survive a winter in the northeastern United States or a humid summer in the South is very challenging.

If you've tried to find good information on growing lavender, particularly its culture, you've probably found that advice can be contradictory and generally all over the place. Its needs are rather complex, and while they may seem simple enough—especially when listed on a nursery label—they are often different based on where your climate.

I am determined to clear the air on the whole lavender issue. Here is just about everything you need to know to master (or kill!) lavender.

◄ The Lavender border, at Wave Hill in the Bronx, New York, runs along a scalding hot gravel path, which is a 'Hell strip'. This impressive border bakes in the summer sunshine, and more importantly, the bed is sited on a well-drained hillside with the benefit of being well-drained in the winter.

FINDING GOOD LAVENDER PLANTS

Often the easiest way to fail with lavender is to go to a garden center or nursery and buy the largest, or what appears to be the healthiest and bushiest, lavender plants you find. The commercial horticulture trade knows that people look for bushy and full lavender each spring, and because of this, plants are produced to look beautiful at the time you will be making a buying decision. The next time you are at a garden center, look around and notice what others are buying. More often than not, their carts will be full of healthy-looking perennials in bud or full bloom. These often have older gray foliage and very dense rootballs and plenty of woody stems, yet lots of new growth may seem to be starting. Take a pass on these and look for small but healthy plants that have not begun to flower.

Lavender is botanically considered to be a small Mediterranean shrub. It comes in several species, some hardier than others. Just asking for lavender or buying something with a label that says "lavender" on it should raise flags with any buyer. Knowing exactly what species, type, or variety of lavender will grow for you is also confusing for many. Just depending on the plant label or advice from an online source or even the grower isn't always helpful, for more often than not, you will see a branded variety sold as "better," "more hardy," or "improved."

Others may look for a variety that sounds like something they want. "French lavender," "English lavender," and "Provence" are all names we will often see associated with lavender. While they all sound desirable, they don't tell you what will grow for you year after year.

Buying Tips

Here are a few pointers on choosing the right plant when it comes to lavender.

- Variety matters, as there are a number of species (or types) of lavender.

- Most lavender sold in the northern United States in spring came from somewhere in the southern states or was raised in a greenhouse from plugs.

- Small specialty nurseries often will have the best plant material for you, as they have propagated their plants or kept them over the winter in their own hoop houses.

- Choose a small plant, singly planted, in a 4-inch (10-cm) pot, not in bud or in bloom if you can find it.

- Avoid pots with three or more cuttings (growers do this to increase the apparent fullness of a specimen plant).

An excellent place to start looking for suitable varieties may be your local flower farmer or maybe even a commercial lavender farmer. There are many today. If you live in England, France, Chile, Australia, or California, you can probably grow most of the lavender varieties without fear or fuss. But you might be surprised to learn that some of the largest lavender farms are emerging on Long Island, New York, Pennsylvania, and Ohio in the United States, so all is not lost. Just know that these growers are planting fields of lavender of particular species and strains, often in raised beds and in locations with breezes and perhaps some winter protection.

SOIL PH

Lavender grows best in alkaline soil, enjoying a pH higher than normal in much of the eastern United States. It can access the nutrients it needs and produce the deepest roots in soil with a pH between 6.8 and 7.0. If your landscape designer set out a dozen plants into garden soil without testing it, your lavender won't die, but it may not thrive or survive long in acid soils.

WATER

Contrary to what most will tell you, lavender enjoys plenty of water. What it does demand is that the water drains off very well. It will not tolerate its roots sitting in soaking wet, muddy, or cold, wet soil, especially in winter when the plants are not growing. Lavender farms—even in the Northeast—irrigate their fields regularly in the summer, but they also grow their lavender in raised beds and in soil that has been amended with a high level of sand or grit so that while some water remains in the soil for the roots to take up, most of it drains off quickly.

PLANT SPACING

Spacing plants far enough apart, away from other plants, is often not practiced, but it should be. Lavender farms grow lavender as a monoculture, spacing plants as far away as 3 to 4 feet (1 to 1.2 m), depending on the variety. It is botanically a tender shrub and biologically designed with dusky, gray foliage to handle hot and dry Mediterranean summers. The foliage, as with many Mediterranean plants, is slightly fuzzy to absorb water from morning dew or from morning maritime air, while the gray, fuzzy leaves help shade the leaf surface from ultraviolet light.

PROFESSIONAL GROWERS

Professionals grow their lavender from rooted cuttings, and the best way for home growers to ensure success is to take cuttings very fall to save over winter. Commercial growers keep their 1-gallon (3.8 L) and 5-gallon (19 L) nursery plants in hoop houses where the pots never freeze, which tips us off on what these plants like.

Young Lavender (*L. angustifolia*)

SPECIES AND VARIETIES

Botanists have identified nearly 50 species of lavender (the genus *Lavandula*), but only a handful are considered to be of horticultural merit for home gardeners. A member of the mint family, most are native to the Mediterranean areas extending from the Canary Islands east throughout the Mediterranean basin, with a few species hailing from southeast India and China.

Lavender has been cultivated since antiquity, both as a medicinal herb and more recently as a culinary one. Lavender oil production for the perfume industry is big business in areas where it grows quickly, and it is also used in modern herbalism.

As an ornamental plant, the genus is highly prized for its grayish foliage. I even consider it a lifestyle plant that can set a tone in the garden, adding romance and visual style to any garden.

Recently, breeders have been able to introduce some new hybrids that you may have heard of, such as 'Phenomenal' or 'Melissa Lilac' that are both cold tolerant to 10°F (-12°C) but can also withstand humid summers.

FRENCH LAVENDER (*L. intermedia*). 'Phenomenal PP24193'. If it snows where you live and if the winters are cold and sometimes wet with unpredictable spring weather, you are somewhat limited in the types of lavender you can grow. You can still grow it, but you need to pay attention to the variety and type you choose. You may have heard about a new "hardier" lavender called Phenomenal, which was introduced a few years ago. You may also have discovered that while Phenomenal was the recommended choice for your climate, the plants still died. Nevertheless, if you've had trouble growing lavender, Phenomenal can indeed be phenomenal. You need to site and space the plants properly, amend the soil for the proper pH and good drainage, and protect it through the winter with a floating row cover. This may not always be the first choice for homes landscaped beautifully, but for most, this will ensure the best results.

Phenomenal is a hybrid selection known for its exceptional cold hardiness and tolerance of summer heat and humidity, as well as its success in winter-wet climates. For zones 5 through 9, it grows best in areas with less than 40 inches (1 m) of rainfall but can withstand more with amended, well-drained soil.

'GROS BLEU'. A choice French lavender that many believe is the finest of modern French hybrids. A tighter grower than most French types, its scent is said to have less camphor and thus smells even sweeter.

SPANISH LAVENDER (*L. stoechas*). One of the lavenders that, while lovely, doesn't look like any of the other lavenders. A fine addition to the herb garden though, with dentate leaves that are silvery and more abundant blossoms with less fragrance.

DUTCH LAVENDER. You will sometimes see this listed as *L. × intermedia* or *L. × angustifolia*, especially from essential oil sources or the holistic medical community, which sometimes get the botany wrong.

Note: Interspecific Crosses

These are named cultivars of interspecific crosses (between two distinct species), particularly *L. × intermedia* (English lavender crosses) and *L. latifolia* from the Iberian Peninsula. These are the hardiest for many gardeners, to at least zone 5, with excellent drainage. We know these more by their varietal names, such as Provence or Grosso, which have been commercially marketed for decades and are excellent garden performers.

ENGLISH LAVENDER (*L. angustifolia*, syn *L. officinalis*). English lavender is a venerable species often referred to as "true lavender."

Tips for Mastering Lavender

Well-draining soil. Lavender likes sandy but not dry soil, ideally elevated on a ridge or in a bed.

Full sun. The more hours per day lavender gets sunshine, the better.

Slightly alkaline soil. Lavender struggles in rich, acidic soil, growing best in soil with a pH between 6.5 and 7.5. Add lime chips or ground limestone annually and at planting.

Variety matters. Choose the right variety for your region. Accept the fact that you may need to grow an English lavender over a French lavender.

Plant early. Plant small plants in early spring rather than later in summer or autumn to ensure proper root development.

Think small. Choose smaller plants over older (woody) plants, as these will be more vigorous.

Space plants far apart. Lavender plants should be 2 to 3 feet (61 cm to 1.2 m) apart, with no neighbors.

Rock mulch. Use gravel mulch (never a wood-bark mulch). This will add heat and evaporate surface moisture on foliage in summer and help raise the temperature in the winter.

Water early. Water your lavender early in the day so the foliage can dry off by night.

Fertility. Lavender is a light feeder, but take a tip from the pros and use a slow-release fertilizer—long and slow is best.

Use a row cover. Protect the dormant plants in winter with a thick floating row cover in winter to dramatically increase the chance that plants will survive by creating a microclimate a few zones warmer. This is standard practice on the East Coast and Canadian lavender farms where winters are snowy or wet, such as in Ontario. Keep the plants covered until hard freezes have passed.

Prune at the right time. In spring, once growth has begun, some cutting back of dead portions of plants is okay, but the proper time to prune away excessive woody growth is after the first flush of bloom.

LESS COMMON BUT VIABLE LAVENDER OPTIONS

- Munstead'

- 'Hidcote Blue' English lavender (*L. angustifolia*) is the best choice of the older selections.

- 'Royal Velvet'

- 'Mitcham Gray'

- 'Jean Davis' is a pale-pink-flowered lavender.

WISTERIA

Wisteria spp.

It's a Hollywood cliché: the sun-soaked Tuscan villa surrounded by fields of lavender, dotted with potted lemon trees set in a neatly clipped boxwood parterre and—hopefully—a wisteria-draped pergola dripping with pendant racemes of fragrant violet flowers. I mean, who wouldn't want that greeting them on a sunny morning?

Sadly, the reality of such a garden often requires a half-dozen full-time gardeners (not to mention that villa in Tuscany!), but so many people dream of that heart-stopping wisteria vine in full bloom. Yet we rarely see one well grown. Why is that? If you've ever tried to grow wisteria, then you know the realities of managing such a scene. While lovely in bloom and even when bare, with its muscular and architectural trunks, there is no getting around the matter that wisteria can often be a thug.

Yet thugness should be no reason for denying yourself this beauty, for how can anyone really live without wisteria in the late spring? I happen to love wisteria and will never have a garden without it, but keeping a wisteria in check requires discipline and perhaps even bondage. I understand if the relationship isn't for everybody. Like keeping a cat from tearing up the sofa to training a terrier to ignore the FedEx driver, wisteria requires a firm hand now and then.

This should come as no surprise to the serious gardener though, as wisteria is a vine, and no vine is well behaved. Their nature is to run wild and to reach for the stars (or the gutters). While vines have their disadvantages, most reward us with something (remember wine?), so while many garden writers may wish to discourage the use of any vine, I say go for it, especially when the gift is something like wisteria's long and luxurious flowers.

◀ White Chinese wisteria (*W. sinensis*) is fragrant, a bit like orange blossoms and hay. Their scent floats across our garden on warm, early summer evenings, and they have the good habit of producing flowers before the foliage fully leafs out.

WISTERIA VARIETIES

If you are into botanical Latin, wisteria can confuse: *Wisteria brachybotrys* sounds a lot like *W. macrobotrys*, not to mention *W. macrostachya* or *W. brachystachya*. (I don't want to confuse you, but there is no such plant as *W. brachystachya*. Nevertheless, you will find it if you enter it into an Internet search window.) It's easier to understand the differences once you know the etymology of the botanic Latin. In this case, *brachy* is from the Greek, meaning "short," while *macro* means "large." As for *stachya*, it too comes from Greek and refers to the overall shape of the inflorescence. Translated literally, it means "spike-like raceme" or "like an ear of grain," such as wheat or corn.

My point is, pay attention to the botanical Latin name. Many popular plants develop synonyms over time (like heirloom tomatoes), and you do want to be certain that you are getting the variety that you want. The wrong wisteria can become a terrible garden menace, if not a thug.

Blooming time helps too, so I organized the species below by blooming sequence, which begins with *W. brachybotrys* (*W. venusta*) in week one, followed by *W. floribunda macrobotrys* (also from Japan) and *W. sinensis* (Chinese wisteria varieties) in week two. Next come the other Japanese wisterias, *W. floribunda*, in week three, followed by the North American natives *W. macrostachya* (Kentucky wisteria) and *W. frutecens* in week four. Chinese wisterias bloom before the foliage emerges, Japanese species bloom at about the same time as the foliage begins to emerge, and North American species bloom after the foliage has emerged. All of this effects how you may want your planting to look.

Wisteria, while rarely grown, is one of those flowers so common that it's more likely that non-gardeners will default to a generic idea of a variety, not unlike we tend to do with lilac or forsythia. It is more common to ask for the "purple wisteria" versus the "white one."

Wisteria floribunda 'Issai'

Selecting a good variety can be challenging, for the Internet is full of fake varieties. One search revealed over 5,000 results, a good sign that a plant is promiscuous or produces plenty of seed. Entrepreneurs may think that they have hit the lottery once they discover that people will pay for romantic flowers, but shop wisely. Just as there isn't a truly blue rose, there isn't a truly blue wisteria other than those found illustrated in Maxfield Parrish prints and on wallpaper.

When it comes to wisteria varieties, you want the best that money can buy, for with that comes behavior, genetics, and good breeding. You will want a triple crown winner with wisteria—one that flowers before the foliage matures and is a profuse bloomer so it will cover a trellis or arbor with long, graceful trusses. Finally, start with a wisteria that was grafted correctly, as this will ensure that the variety you invested in is indeed the proper color and strain.

GETTING WISTERIA TO BLOOM

Stubborn vines that don't bloom are either not mature enough (wisteria needs to be 15 years old to bloom, or even older with some species) or they need to be carefully tricked into believing that they are more mature. You can achieve this through stress. Carefully cut the bark vertically in 1-inch (2.5-cm) vertical slits every inch around the diameter of the trunk. This will damage part of the cambium layer, but it does stimulate a stress situation that can cause the vine to bloom. It may sound drastic, but cutting is still practiced in Italy and on some European estates, where it is documented to have worked for some growers.

TRAINING WISTERIA

When training wisteria on a structure, you may be tempted to help the plant by hand-winding stems a certain way. Understand that each wisteria has a unique habit of twining that is specific to its species. *W. sinensis*, *W. brachybotrys*, and both American species (*W. frutescens* and *W. macrostachya*) naturally twine counterclockwise, and no attempt to get the vines to twine clockwise will work.

W. floribunda, however, wants to grow in a clockwise pattern. You might think that this has something to do with the Southern and Northern Hemispheres, but it doesn't. Each Japanese species twines in a different pattern too. It's just interesting to know and helpful when training a plant to avoid interruptions in a pattern you may be trying to achieve.

Lastly, when training wisteria, know that every stem can and will grow into a thick, muscular trunk if left to mature. While the wisteria is young, be mindful of how you train the primary trunks. As they grow, they will thicken, becoming woody and covered in bark. A 10-year vine can have a trunk as thick as a tree. As such, training is necessary for the structure of the plant. But also pay attention to the structure it is being trained upon and make sure that it is strong enough for the eventual elephantine trunks that will develop. I've lost plenty of wooden trellises once those wimpy wisteria stems became swole. A good trick is to imagine each stem transforming into a python-thick trunk within just a few years. Plan accordingly as you guide young stems, especially in and out of wooden lathe or around a pole.

If using a wood trellis or support, invest in mahogany or cedar at least 6 inches (15 cm) in diameter. Remember that eventually it's the structure that decays, never the wisteria vine itself. In fact, this is how the fabled and desirable "wisteria trees" came about. They are vines trained to a stake will rot when the wisteria is strong enough to stand on its own.

WISTERIA PRUNING

Knowing what can go wrong with wisteria and being prepared for it is half the battle. Wisteria is a vine that can grow nearly 16 feet (4.9 m) a year if left untended, so do not ever leave a wisteria untended. That said, a fierce pruning and trimming should need to happen only a few times a year, including a spring cut back to remove winter kill and to encourage the flower buds to emerge, and then a mid-summer wisteria-scaping. Errant whips and long runners can and will take over a structure or nearby tree in just a matter of days if not checked.

Be conscious while pruning. You don't want to be too aggressive with the secateurs, especially later in the season as flower buds could be damaged or removed. The wood where flower buds will form next spring happens on spurs, much like with apple trees. Herein lies one of the great problems with wisteria—getting them to bloom on command. Or getting them to bloom at all for some people.

WISTERIA-SCAPING

- Trim back long whips and aggressive growth in midsummer, a month or two after blooming.

- Cut back any other aggressive or inappropriate growth in late autumn once the leaves have dropped.

- Remove seedpods at any time. Though they can be attractive, it is best to cut them off in early autumn before they burst open to reduce self-seeding.

- Avoid cutting any stems where the current year's growth emerged from the previous year's growth, as this is where flower buds will form the following spring.

WISTERIA TREES

One alternative to training wisteria on a trellis or an arbor is to train it into a self-supporting (eventually) tree shape. A vine trained into a tree shape will take some time, years even, to be strong enough to stand on its own. Older vines can still have some support, such as a sturdy metal pole, which eventually becomes hidden as the trunk develops and swells around it.

A wisteria trained into a tree shape doesn't require any more work than one climbing a trellis or arbor. Note that "tree" here means 5 to 6 feet (1.5 to 1.8 m) tall, as there is no such thing as a wisteria that grows like a tree naturally. Essentially forming a wisteria tree involves training a vigorous vine to grow like a lollipop topiary. The result after 10 years or so of training will be an extraordinary enhancement to the garden. I find that shorter wisteria trees look better in a landscape than taller ones (6 to 9 feet [1.8 to 2.7 m]), and they are easier to get into with hand pruners. As these will require frequent trimming to keep them neat, always be conscious about last season's wood and the spurs where new stems emerge, holding at least 6 inches (15 cm) of current-year wood so that you will have plenty of flowers next year.

Once grown only on estates with skilled full-time gardeners, a wisteria tree today can be had for what many will consider a good investment, but it is just that—an investment. A wisteria tree not only is long-lived, but it also inevitably gets better with age. There are some over 80 years old in gardens that I know.

A trained 'tree wisteria' is just a vine that has been trained to a stake and pruned heavily. In 5-8 years the stake could be removed.

AUTUMN BLOOMS

I can say this because I've worked in the commercial design world for 30 years: autumn has been hijacked by designers. I'm all for decorating and celebrating the seasons, but I'm even more for being accurate. Humans have been celebrating the fall harvest season for centuries, yet as a plantsman and a gardener, I know that horticulturally there is much more to expressing autumn than corn mazes, pumpkin spice, and apple picking.

Just a century ago, tall Japanese chrysanthemums showcased in elaborate displays in the conservatories and botanic gardens of the Victorian era marked the fall season. Nature herself celebrates this vernal change beautifully around our planet. From camellias that bloom in the mountains of Korea to the many bulbs that blossom in response to fall rains and cooler temperatures, it is a rich and varied growing season.

Gardeners know exactly what "harvest" means. It means towers of colorful heirloom pumpkins, hundreds of old apple varieties, a rainbow of dried beans, digging potatoes, and planting foxgloves and hollyhocks that we started in July for blooming the following year.

For us, autumn doesn't follow the standard style guide provided to retailers, as so many flowers during this season are indeed off palette. Purple, pink, white, and red flowers challenge the assumption that fall is expressed only with orange, brown, and gold. In our garden, autumn is a season when pots of October-blooming pink camellias contrast nicely with the orange leaves of sugar maples. It's when nerine bulbs in the greenhouse start to bloom in every shade of pink and red. It's when tall Japanese chrysanthemums begin to come into bloom—mums that barely resemble the chemically stunted mounds of hardy mums omnipresent at farmstands and home centers.

◀ A 150 years ago chrysanthemums were considered connoisseur flowers, grown for autumnal conservatory displays where they were trained to achieve fantastic forms. On the brink of extinction, a new generation of flower lovers are rediscovering (and saving) these aristocrats of the floral world.

ABOVE: Japanese and exhibition chrysanthemums on our back porch in October.

RIGHT: 'Croydon Masterpiece' dahlia was introduced in 1948 and still wins shows and our hearts when it is offered by flower farmers. As a garden plant, it has large dinner-plate sized bloom, so be sure to stake it well.

LEFT: If each stem is disbudded by just a single bud and well staked, a formal ball form like this 'Skipley Lois Jean' can grow as large as a softball and win its class at a dahlia show.

ABOVE: Japanese and exhibition mums bloom late from cutting started outdoors in June. I like to display them in the greenhouse for late autumn parties with vintage Japanese-inspired paper lanterns from antique shops to add to the 19th-century feel.

ABOVE: 'Derek Bircumshaw' is a vibrant, deep, golden yellow mum from the Regular Incurve class. Popular with Chrysanthemum Society exhibitors both in the US and the UK, if disbudded it produces a large flower that will brighten a late October garden or porch display.

RIGHT: 'Cornel Bronze' is a popular ball-form dahlia with cut flower farmers, but it can also be a good exhibition flower. Leave the plant alone, just stake it, and you'll harvest armloads of smaller cut flowers. Yet prune it to three or five stems and remove side buds, and each blossom can grow to 4 or 5 inches (10 cm or 13 cm) in diameter.

LEFT: 'A mixed border of dahlias on the walk leading to the greenhouse include some of the more unusal classes like anemone flowers and collerettes. Red and white 'Wowie' is always a standout.

ABOVE: Mocha is a giant spider form popular in autumn displays if trained to a singe or three-stemmed plant.

DAHLIA

Dahlia

Welcome back, dahlias! Few flowers have made such a sensational and spectacular comeback in recent years as the dahlia. Considered by many to be too showy and old-fashioned just 20 years ago, the dahlia has bounced back bigger and better than anyone could have imagined. When I would give summer bulb lectures in garden clubs in the late 1990s, the audience would laugh and groan when I showed slides of dahlias. But like all trends, things cycle back into fashion. Today, dahlias are sought after by gardeners of all ages and generations.

Dahlia lovers know that there is tremendous diversity among the many groups of dahlias, and honestly, there is a dahlia type for almost every taste and style. The American Dahlia Society (ADS) recognizes 29 forms of dahlias. That means that there are 29 basic shapes to the flowers, but it doesn't end there. Enthusiasts have grouped all the dahlia types and forms by applying a complex organizational principle and have created charts and codes. Exhibitors use these codes as they bench their dahlia blossoms at dahlia society shows. The letters and numbers inform everyone of the form, size, and color of each and every dahlia. As a home gardener, you don't need to know any of these, but some basic knowledge of the system

◀ Cut flower farms are a great source for building a list of dahlias with long stems and upright blooms that are good for arranging in the house. Clockwise from top left: 'Chimacum Doris', 'Hollyhill Miss White', 'Formby Art', 'Snoho Doris', 'Café Au Lait', and 'Valley Rust Bucket'

Dahlia 'Hollyhill Calico' a miniature ball but grown on a plant that can reach 6 feet (1.8 m) tall.

is helpful, especially if you plan to buy some of the genuinely spectacular dahlias found online from specialty growers. Detailed information can also be found on the ADS.com website, just in case you want to become even more dahlia-literate.

So with 29 basic forms, there is a lot to know about dahlias. For example, while you may think that you know what a cactus dahlia looks like, did you know that there are three distinct classifications of cactus? Each one is not only quite different, but also the cactus form itself can appear on many other sizes of dahlia. For another example, take the dahlias many of us call "dinner plates." The giant 12- to 14-inch (30- to 36-cm) flowers are the stars of dahlia shows. However, the term "dinner plate" is never used by dahlia society members; instead, they call them "AA" or "giant."

TODAY'S DAHLIAS

"Cutflower dahlias," "garden dahlias," and "exhibition dahlias" are categories you often see mentioned in good dahlia catalogs and descriptions. While there isn't a clear definition for each term, it's good to know if the dahlia you are considering is an excellent garden or landscape dahlia or if it has characteristics like long stem length and no leaves that make it suitable for a cut flower. Some dahlias are known for their performance in the garden but aren't good exhibition or even cutflower dahlias.

Some of the greatest garden dahlias have dark-tinted foliage. One favorite with garden designers is 'David Howard', a lovely, dark-leaved variety that produces lots of ball-shaped flowers that are a buffy tangerine color and complement many other flowers when set in the garden. Another dark-foliage dahlia is 'Bishop of Llandaff', a red-flowered single variety. Many new dark-leaved selections are being introduced annually.

There have been many advancements in breeding new garden-worthy dahlias. Recently some hot, trendy dahlias have come along, some of which surprised dahlia connoisseurs. Among them is 'Cafe au Lait', an old variety that was developed in the 1960s and always got a bad rap despite its magical color because its flowers were too loosely structured. The 'Cafe au Lait' lingered modestly in the gardens of those who loved it until a *Martha Stewart Weddings* photographer and stylist featured it. Overnight, it not only became popular, it went viral. Suddenly every stylish bride wanted the buffy–pale pink irregular flower in their bouquets, and the few dahlia tuber sites that still bothered to grow and carry the tubers were shocked when it sold out in just a few days.

Mixed dahlias from our late summer garden.

Growing dahlias in a separate bed dedicated only to dahlias allows one to stake them securely without worrying about how they look. With wide paths between rows and few plants nearby to compete or share, dahlias can be fed, pruned, and tended to properly.

Most serious dahlia growers relegate the flowers to rows either in the vegetable garden, where they can be staked like tomatoes, or a separate garden dedicated to dahlias. This has its benefits, as all dahlias will need to be staked with 2 × 2 lumber or steel rods, which can be unattractive in the border. An unstaked dahlia is a disaster waiting to happen. That said, dahlias work well in a garden as long as you understand that they will bloom later in the season. They should be planted with adequate space around them so that they can get all the light and nutrients they need while growing. Imagine them much as you would a tomato plant (you would never plant a tomato plant between a phlox and a large peony in a perennial border). All the blooms will be near the top of the plant. With some planning, however—small dahlias to the front of a bed and tall ones planted in the rear—a border of only dahlias can be a sensation in early fall. In mixed borders, dahlias also look beautiful, especially if you plant mid-tier plants like zinnias and salvias in front of them to cover the lower parts of the plants, which can be unattractive near blooming time.

Most dahlias grow very well in containers, which surprises many new gardeners. Even the very large dinner plates and tall pompoms can be successfully grown in large pots if they are staked properly, with 6-foot (1.8-m) bamboo canes in the tallest pots. Many dahlia exhibitors grow their plants in containers if they have little space, and even the smallest deck or terrace can house a few miniature dahlias in 8-inch (20-cm) pots.

Give dahlia tubers a head-start under lights or in a greenhouse.

Transplant outdoors only after your frost-free date.

Staking with strong posts is essential to avoid broken stems.

HOW TO GROW DAHLIAS

Dahlias are so hot right now that often the best color and varieties sell out quickly. In response, some dahlia sellers announce a release date and time when their tubers go on sale, so watch for these events. Always order as early as you can, sometimes as early as late summer or autumn in the previous year, as this is when many serious growers order their tubers, often before their current plants have begun to bloom. If you are more flexible, dahlia tubers are always available right up to late spring by the larger growers, and since there is no lousy dahlia from the gardener's perspective, never think that it is too late. Just keep in mind that a hot variety will sell out quicker than a limited-edition pair of designer shoes.

Dahlias are easy to grow and can be started many different ways, including seeds, tubers, and cuttings. Planting tubers is the best way to start dahlias. You can usually find tubers at garden centers in the spring, but for the really great varieties, look to catalogs and websites from professional dahlia nurseries. These include flower farms that often sell a portion of their stock off every spring.

Tubers are shipped dormant, but if you order them in late spring, there is always a risk that a few may start producing stems, so be careful when unpacking them. It is recommended that you start your dahlia plants indoors early, 3 to 6 weeks before you plan to put them in the ground. Wait to put them outside until the soil has warmed to at least 60°F (16°C). Setting tubers out into cold soil risks rot. Bright light is essential when starting tubers. Plant the tubers in small pots just larger than the size of the tuber (usually a 3- or 4-inch [8- to 10-cm] pot) with the stem just emerging from the pot. Use sterile potting mix and not garden compost. If you don't have a greenhouse or an artificial light setup, set out small pots in a protected area, such as a deck or terrace a few weeks before you plan to plant.

Dahlia tubers vary in size, and their size has little to do with a plant's vigor or future size. Don't be surprised if you get one giant tuber, a few mediocre ones, and a tiny one if ordering various varieties. Dahlia tubers don't behave the same as other tubers like potatoes. New growth will not emerge randomly or from eyes around the tuber but instead will emerge on the portion of the tuber where a tiny part of last year's stem was attached. If you break a tuber in

DAHLIA CULTURE

START: Start tubers indoors under lights 3 to 5 weeks early.

PLANT: Plant outdoors after the last frost.

PINCH: Pinch new growth at the second pair of leaves.

SOIL: Create rich, fertile loam with additional compost.

STAKE: Add strong stakes before plants get too tall.

FEED: Dahlias respond well to high nutrition. Use low-nitrogen organic fertilizer and develop high organic matter.

WATER: Dahlias need lots of water for those celery-like stems. Irrigate in the morning to avoid fungal problems.

DISBUD: Serious growers remove side buds, leaving one per stem for the highest quality flowers.

DIG UP TUBERS: Wait 1 week after a killing frost before digging clumps. Cut, wash, and label tubers all in one day.

STORE TUBERS: Store entire clumps wrapped in newspaper or individual tubers in vermiculite or wood shavings in a cold (38°F to 48°F [3°C to 9°C]) place that does not freeze.

Wait a few days after frost kills the foliage before digging clumps. This properly cures the tubers and allows you to see where the 'eyes' are if you are dividing in the fall.

Dividing dahlias in the fall is an art but is the preferred method. Wash to remove soil, then cut with a sterile knife always retaining part of the original stem attached to the tuber. Discard all others.

Each of these tubers ready for storage has at least one eye on the stem end. 'Eye's' will disappear in a few weeks making dividing clumps more challenging if you wait.

Flower farmers and dahlia society exhibitors protect their dahlias from insect damage and those nasty, hidden earwigs not with insecticides, but by outsmarting them. Growers rely on organza gift bags (purchased online from wedding supply sites) that allow sun and air in, but not pests. Tie them on as buds swell using the ribbons they come with (especially for white dahlias), and remove them when you cut the flowers for arrangements.

(5 cm) of water a week when flowers are forming. Daily monitoring of plants is encouraged.

STAKING AND PRUNING

The biggest chore when growing dahlias is keeping up with adequate staking. Experience will teach you the hard way that dahlias need strong stakes, at least a 1 × 1-inch (2.5 × 2.5-cm), 6-foot (1.8-m)–tall stakes or three 1-inch (2.5-cm) bamboo canes set in a circle around each plant. Weekly tying and management of stems is necessary, but exactly how much you need to do depends on the variety and what you are growing dahlias for. Staking becomes the only chore in late summer and, even then, the few stems that seem to grow so quickly in autumn will snap off during a heavy rainstorm. So never skimp on staking and staking materials. A wet dahlia blossom can be as heavy as a head of iceberg lettuce positioned on a stem as strong as that of a zinnia.

Pruning or stem removal will help most dahlias. Advanced growers pinch plants at the time of planting and then remove all but three main stems by midsummer. Since new stems will form at nearly every leaf axil, most growers leave one stem per leaf axil and remove the opposite one. Remember you are growing dahlias more for the flowers or garden display than for foliage.

half, discard the bottom piece, as it will never grow a stem, but the stem end generally will survive and sprout. Serious growers sometimes cut overly large tubers in half, planting only the stem end after the cut has healed.

AMENDMENTS

Dahlias are robust feeders and respond well to both organic and inorganic fertilizer. Manure is useful in early spring, or enriched soil the previous autumn with fresh stable manure and straw bedding. Do not apply manure in early spring as it is high in nitrogen, which will generate lush growth and foliage at the expense of flowers. Most dahlia growers use a low-nitrogen N-P-K formula such as 3-5-5. Mulch will help with irrigation, since dahlias consume at least 2 inches

DISBUDDING

All exhibition dahlias are disbudded, which means that all the flower buds are removed from a stem except the single one in the center top of the stem. This will focus all of the plant's energy on producing a single, large, and perfect blossom. With just a twist of the forefinger and thumb, the smaller side buds can be removed. Disbudding any later risks leaving a scar on the stem. As a home grower, I encourage you to experiment with disbudding on multiple varieties. I like to disbud some plants but not others, which gives me a wide range of blossom sizes.

The concept of disbudding is more about producing the largest, most perfect flower. Competitive growers who show the big dinner plate (AA) dahlias grow just a single flower per plant or stem, removing all but one central bud.

So if you want to try to get that 14-inch (36-cm)–diameter monster, the more you prune and disbud, the higher the chance. I disbud about half of my cutflower dahlias and all of my competition dahlias, but there comes a time when it's all just too much work and the dahlias get the best of you.

DIGGING AND STORING TUBERS

Storing dahlias is always a hot topic at dahlia society lecture meetings. Gather 10 dahlia growers in a room though and most will have devised their own method for saving tubers. There are so many ways to store dahlias that it is hard to suggest just one way, but I can review a few of the most common methods and how I do it. First of all, you should know that to survive winter, a dahlia tuber needs just enough moisture so that it won't wither and dry up but not so much that it rots. It also wants to be cool, if not cold, yet never freezing.

A hundred years ago, it was much easier to keep dahlia tubers over the winter, as people had storage rooms, unheated barns, and root cellars. Our house is 120 years old, and I keep dahlias where my grandparents kept theirs: in our cork-lined storeroom in the basement where part of the floor is bare dirt. It's also where we store potatoes and canned goods as well, but this is a set of environmental conditions few people have today.

Roger Swain, former host of PBS's *The Victory Garden*, once told me that the best way to store dahlia tubers was to dig out clumps, sometimes taking the entire rootball with the undivided tubers, wrap the clumps in newspaper, set them in a taped cardboard box, and then store the entire box in a dirt-floored farmhouse cellar. Again, not precisely what most of us have access to, but this does provide us some hints as to what the tubers need: darkness, enough moisture so that they don't desiccate, and cold temperatures just above freezing. The newspaper functions like a sponge, absorbing a bit of moisture but also keeping just enough dampness in the remaining soil in the clump to get it through the winter.

Dahlias should never be dug until they've been first hit by frost. Once frost freezes the foliage, cut the tall stems back. You can cut stems to any length, usually leaving a few inches (cm) near the base of the plant as a handle.

Leave the rootball in the ground for a week to cure. When you dig them up, you have two options. The first is to wash the soil off the rootball and then cut and divide the tubers. With a sharp knife and a cutting board, begin dissecting, first by cutting the main stem down to about 1 inch (2.5 cm), and then cutting the stem like a pie so that a portion of the stem is attached to the best tubers. Not all of the tubers will be viable, as some only attach to the old stem with a thread-like root. These should be discarded. You should end up with 5 to 10 tubers per plant. These can be labeled with a waterproof marker right on the tuber, or you can make a new label to store with the cut tubers.

The tidiest way to store cut tubers is in a plastic shoebox filled with some dry organic material, such as dry potting mix, wood shavings, or vermiculite. Include the label or write the variety on the box itself, and store the entire box in the coolest spot you have that does not freeze, perhaps a mudroom or a breezeway, striving for that ideal 48°F (9°C) maximum.

You can also keep the rootball intact (still with some soil on it, which will help the root ball retain some moisture through the winter). Some wrap the rootball in newspaper and store it in a cardboard box in a cool cellar. Others set the rootballs in trash barrels filled with dry autumn leaves or in plastic trash bags filled with leaves, kept open at the top. Most every grower has their own secret method for storing dahlias.

My method is a lazy method. While I do cut and save some of my more expensive dahlias in the autumn (I store cut tubers in vermiculite-filled plastic shoe boxes), most of my other dahlias are simply dug up in their entirety and set into black plastic bulb crates, which I keep under the benches in my greenhouse. I divide all of these in late winter just before they begin to sprout.

GLADIOLUS

Gladiolus spp.

Right or wrong, we make many assumptions about common flowers like the chrysanthemum and the carnation, but the gladiolus may suffer the most from a PR standpoint. It is often referred to as the "funeral flower" and is widely regarded as an inexpensive filler flower for florists. While both accounts are correct in practice, the genus *Gladiolus* has a long and interesting history in horticulture.

Gladiolus includes nearly 300 species found mostly found in South Africa, but it also includes a few Mediterranean species that have naturalized in agricultural fields in milder parts of southern Europe. What most of us think of as a gladiolus, or gladiola, today is quite different than any of the wild species. Their development is well documented and extends from the earliest species imported from South Africa by Dutch and English ships around 1740. The very first collected species to reach Europe are still grown as useful mild-winter garden plants or as summer-growing potted plants in colder climates with greenhouses. Among these are *G. alatus*, *G. blandus*, and the highly fragrant *G. tristis*, all of which are becoming popular again with plant collectors looking for something different.

If you love intense fragrance, *G.tristis* is for you. Native to South Africa, it typically blooms in winter for me (as it comes from the Southern Hemisphere). New crosses are being introduced as a garden plant (look for varieties called 'Buttery cheeks' or 'Peachy Cheeks'. Hardy to zone 7 they open up new channels for summer blooming bulbs for mild climates.

◀ Gladiolus corms are often inexpensive and even a mix of bad corms will produce flowers like this.

The large, colorful hybrid *Gladiolus* we are most familiar with today really didn't become popular until the late 19th century, well after dozens of species were grown by collectors in both Europe and the United States. The goal early on was to develop a summer-blooming variety, but most were winter growers (Southern Hemisphere winter-wet conditions). A Belgian gardener named Hermann Josef Bedinghaus made the first cross in 1837, combining *G. psittacinus* and *G. cardinalis*. By 1848 Louis van Houtte listed at least 10 hybrids in his popular bulb catalog, and by 1852, over a hundred varieties had become available throughout Europe from the Netherlands to France and Germany. New species continued to be added to the DNA mix, and even hybrids were being crossed with each other, creating even more complex crosses.

It wasn't until the late 19th century that great nurserymen like Victor Lemoine crossed *G. purpureoauratus* with the older hybrids to create tall, flowering gladiolas like we know today. By the time the 20th century closed, more species were introduced into the breeding mix, and the flower form and color palette began to change. The hooded flower with lips, the typical gladiolus form today, arrived around 1890, and the modern gladiolus really took shape.

HYBRID GLADIOLAS

One could say that hybrid *Gladiolus* are nearly as polarizing as politics. There seems to be no middle ground, but gladiola love is based more on style and fashion trends than anything else: you either hate them (perhaps because of their association with funerals) or you find them beautiful (in a 1930s movie prop sort of way). In my experience, most people fall into the former category. But the hybrid *Gladiolus* is truly an artifact of another era, which is a good way to approach them. While limited as essentially vase flowers, they have a nostalgic quality that may be lost on younger generations. My mother grew full-sized ones for church arrangements as well as miniature ones for tall McCoy vases we would set on our old baby grand piano or side table. If you collect arts and crafts–era pottery or have a few relic Art Deco vases from your great-grandmother in the attic, you have a perfect vessel to display gladiolas.

Many Depression-era urns and antique florist baskets from the 1920s were designed for cutflower gladiolus because they were very popular in the first half of the 20th century. In fact, it's hard to imagine a florist shop in an old black-and-white Hollywood film without a massive arrangement of white gladiolus. They were the Ginger Rogers and Fred Astaire of the floral world.

THE NEW GLADIOLUS

The hybrid *Gladiolus* is being transformed to fit a 21st-century mindset. The flowers are becoming extraordinarily ruffled and noticeably larger, almost orchid-like. But the evolution is really all about new colors. Imagine rusty browns, chestnut and gray speckles, deep merlots and dark violets, mustardy golds, and coral with lime greens. The trend may be reigniting, as I've seen arrangements with these stylish yet odd rusty or pewter tones combined with magnolia foliage in the lobbies of posh boutique hotels in New York City. The look suddenly feels fresh and new.

Gladiolas have always had a unique color palette, with older varieties sometimes coming in amazing tones of deep purples or pure avocado-green flowers. Combinations with contrasting blotches on the bottom lip have been popular in exhibitions, and now that change is happening, slowly, with gladiolus for the home. Most older commercial varieties do still default to the familiar yet harsher tones of fire engine red, sulfur yellow, and pure bubblegum pink. But I predict that once a daring propagator offers volumes of a new color to the market, the flower farmer movement will lead this shift, and later the more desirable gladiolus will eventually make it into rows in our home gardens, just as the dahlia has.

New hybrid gladiolus are being selected for their extreme ruffling and unusual colors that are more stylish then old cultivars. Designers can now choose from many shades of brown, gray, mustard, and plum.

Gladiolus at Gladiolus Society exhibition.

HOW TO GROW GLADIOLUS

Gladiolus are easy to grow, demanding little beyond what's required by a tomato plant. They grow from a corm (not botanically a bulb, but close) that is set deep into the ground in late spring once the weather has warmed to a safe-enough temperature that the native plants have fully leafed out. A trench is dug 6 to 10 inches (16 to 25 cm) deep in loamy soil (like that found in a vegetable garden). Adequate water and good, proper nutrition is vital, especially if you plan to keep the corms that form from year to year. Good drainage is so crucial that some growers lay in a trench with sand and set the corms into this, topping the sand off just at the top of the corm. This is an old technique that works well, as the roots can emerge and reach down to the more fertile soil, keeping the corm dryer. This sort of detail, while often unnecessary for average growers cultivating a few plants as cut flowers, or who plant just a row or two of gladiolus in the vegetable garden, does help culturally, so it is worth the extra effort.

Fertilizer, either organic or inorganic, is essential. So is weeding if you want the plants to grow well and corms of equal or larger size to develop so you can save them over the winter for next year.

The art of growing gladiolus has almost been lost to a multiple-generation gap that has passed between families that raised glads. While technique is low on the difficulty scale, you must follow at least a few basic. First corms should ideally be planted at the exact moment when they break dormancy. A spikey shoot emerging from the top doesn't always indicate that growth has begun, for the basal root scar where the roots appear provides the key information. Roots will begin to force rounded nubs, which is the best indicator of a corm that is ready to go into the ground.

Fertility is usually provided as a balanced feed, as with vegetables. Choose organic or inorganic. Usually a fertilizer slightly lower in nitrogen is used, something like a 5-10-15, as it is a bulb plant. Any fertilizer you may use for tomatoes should be fine. The fertilizer you are providing is helping the formation of next year's corm as well as the flowers this year.

Gladiolus corms organized for planting in May.

Corms

Botanically corms are different than bulbs, as they are what botanists call a "modified stem." What this means is the roots will emerge from the bottom, not unlike an onion, and the spear or shoot will emerge from the top.

A gladiolus corm showing new growth in spring.

STAKING

Gladiolus, particularly the tall standard ones, need staking. In the wild, most gladiolas grow through low-growing brush or tall grasses, so they naturally have a kind of staking around them. In more natural plantings, the species and the closer crosses look very natural if planted out in grassy meadows as a matrix plant or clustered together in a tightly planted perennial border. When you are growing them as a cut flower, supports are needed. The best are usually thin bamboo canes inserted carefully so as not to hit the corm underground. I like to add mine at planting so I know where the row is set out, which helps keep me from stepping on the emerging leaves.

The sword-shaped foliage itself doesn't need any support, but once the flower spike emerges, the stem will need to be tied closely to the bamboo cane. Just be careful not to tie sections of the stem where the flower buds are forming, as this will distort them. Take care to fasten the spike early enough, before wind or rain tips the plant, as you will never be able to straighten out a spike that has decided to grow upward on a tilted plant. Always use soft twine, thin rope, or staking tape; never use coated wire, as this will cut into the stem.

WATERING

At least an inch (2.5 cm) of water a week is essential for a long flower stem to form and to avoid short flower spikes. Even though gladiolus likes water, good drainage is also necessary, as plants will suffer if the soil is too muddy or if corms sit in mucky soil. This is why a raised bed is ideal.

CUTTING FLOWERS

Even though you may want the longest stems, avoid cutting foliage off with your stem, striving to leave at least four leaves that can remain to help feed the corm for next year's bloom. New corms form at the bottom of the old ones, so know that you are primarily feeding the plant to build an entirely new corm, which hopefully will be larger than the one you planted.

DIGGING CORMS

You can lift the entire plant anytime in the late summer or autumn, once the foliage has begun to brown. Always include the label with your extracted plant so you can keep track of varieties. I dig my plants with a pitchfork and shake off some soil, laying the entire plant down in plastic mesh trays that I save from buying annuals in the spring. You will want these plants to continue browning before you cut off the foliage, as the nutrients are still in the leaves. Wait to cut until the plants are completely dried, or cured. I set my corms on a shaded porch out of the direct sun, where there are breezes. You can store yours anywhere they can remain dry with some airflow, such as a shelf in a garage or a shed. Once dry, cut the foliage off, leaving 1 inch (2.5 cm) of the stalk at the top of the corm, and store in a cool, dry place for the winter.

Like dahlias, gladiolus are best grown in a vegetable garden where you don't need to be afraid to cut them. Be sure to stake them, which will be easier to do if you grown them close together in a row like this.

CHRYSANTHEMUM

Chrysanthemum spp.

Most Westerners, when they shop for chrysanthemums, are on the hunt for pots of hardy mums, those dense mounds of million-budded plants that are omnipresent as fall approaches. They are used largely as disposable display plants in autumn motifs, often alongside a scarecrow, a few bales of hay, and some pumpkins, corn stalks, or ornamental kale. At the risk of sounding like a flower elitist, this mum-centered autumn vignette has become a rather tired cliché. What I am going to share with you about mums here has nothing to do with any of this.

Few flowers bring back the past like old-school chrysanthemums, popular still in exhibitions. I love it when I find an old painting in a museum or online that shows an 18th- or 19th-century greenhouse full of chrysanthemums that look almost exactly like my greenhouse looks on a cold November day.

To truly appreciate the chrysanthemum, look back to China. It was there nearly 3,000 years ago that a fan base for the flower and form began to grow, and chrysanthemums were put to use in everything from decorative arts to medicine to horticulture, making it one of the first, if not the first, ornamental plants cultivated by humans.

The chrysanthemum exploded into US culture after World War II, when more people found themselves owning their own home, perhaps with a white picket fence and a little vegetable garden. This cultural shift and new enthusiasm for gardening buoyed the landscape gardening world in total, but the chrysanthemum carved out a unique place, filling the gap between tomato plants and Christmas trees. The hardy mum entered the American panorama. The whole chrysanthemum family became the world's most popular cut flowers due to their ability to survive out of water and the fact that they could be brought into bloom any week of the year just by controlling day length in the growing environment. It remains the most popular cut flower today.

◄ Japanese and exhibition chrysanthemums on display in the greenhouse in early November are a reason for a late garden party as these mums are so rarely seen today in our gardens.

'Flair', a large, orchid pink spider-flowered form can grow 6 feet (18 m) tall if disbudded and trained to a triple stemmed plant.

'Gertrude', a large, irregular incurve can be trained both as a garden mum or disbudded to produce a huge, single flower that blooms in mid-October.

TYPES OF MUMS

All chrysanthemums are marginally hardy, especially if planted earlier in the year so the roots can establish themselves. They are undoubtedly hardy in more moderate climates, such as zones 7 and higher.

HARDY MUMS. The hardy mums you buy in the fall do have their place, but they are limited in that, like most chrysanthemums, they are not cold or winter hardy. Some may survive in zone 5 or lower if planted near a foundation or a large boulder, but they will rarely return. If they do, don't expect a repeat performance. The hardy mums that you buy as fall décor are specially grown with growth regulators to keep them artificially low and squat, which does not improve their longevity, even in temperate climates. However, do cut back plants that manage to survive to a second season at least twice before late summer. This will help them branch and thus ensure more blooms.

Hardy mums are more likely to survive if you are able to get cuttings or young plants in the early summer. These will be able to establish roots that can sustain through a harsh winter better than a rootball that was planted in autumn.

PERENNIAL AND KOREAN MUMS. Some garden strains of hardy mums do make fantastic perennials and are beginning to be offered that way by garden centers, by mail-order nurseries, and at plant sales. Look for varieties like peachy-apricot colored 'Sheffield', 'Venus' (a lavender single), 'Meioko' (a double violet), or 'Ryan's Pink', which forms daisy-like pink flowers that will last nearly until the snow falls. They are all lovely in perennial borders and produce a beautiful effect in the garden, like a well-behaved daisy, but one that blooms just before frost. Often these are the last perennials to bloom, and as such, they get plenty of notice in the garden. Remarkably, very few gardeners know of these plants. They are root hardy to zone 4.

Korean mums should be more widely used by both garden designers and home gardeners. They are best ordered in the late winter from mail-order nurseries so the rooted cuttings or divisions can be planted directly into a perennial border in early spring. In just a single season, a small plant in a 3-inch (8-cm) pot can grow into an impressive giant, and within 3 years, most gardeners will be so delighted with the display that they will pass along cuttings or divisions to their friends. Seeds of some Korean mums are sometimes offered by overseas seed catalogs and are an easy way to grow a collection.

Spoon mums are unique and always popular. 'Fantasy' is basically a daisy with petals that curl to form spooned ends.

The Irregular Incurve form is popular with chrysanthemum growers who exhibit in competitions. I just love these for my home displays on our porches in November when flowers like 'Kokka No Wazza' (from Japan) take over the displays from pumpkins and squash.

PRACTICAL HOME GARDENING

In backyards and home cutting gardens, mums can be as grown as easily as starting with small plants and cuttings and then setting aside an area in which to grow them. They will need staking or netting if you are growing many, as well as some weekly care.

If you are interested in raised mums in the garden or border, choose varieties intended for that purpose. Know that most large-flowered exhibition types, such as spider mums or football types, are not suitable for integrating into mixed borders. If raised in pots somewhere else, they can be set into the ground once trained as long as your climate allows for their very late-season bloom.

I have experimented with all of the exhibition mums and would be lost without growing all of the gnomes or bonsai types, which are usually trained as a sweet little topiary or as quick-growing bonsai trees. They can also be grown as everyday garden plants, as these small-blooming varieties are more natural looking than store-bought hardy mums, and they are naturally dwarf.

These rarely seen Cascade Class of mums can be trained with five cuttings in a 12 inch (30 cm) pot to drape down over and form waterfall of flowers.

Class 12, the Brush and Thistle, form are unique look that resembles brushes or thistles. 'Saga Nishiki' is a popular variety with those who love novelty shapes.

The Reflex form is a favorite of mine, especially if grown to a huge, single flower (by disbudding). The tomato-red color of 'Paint Box' is a color so welcome in autumn.

Since I have a greenhouse, I also love the challenge of raising traditional cascade mums in some years or a collection of tall exhibition single-stem mums more for my own pleasure. Huge spider mums on 6-foot (1.8 m) stems are an annual treat in the greenhouse, and the flowers are also cut for late fall displays along with most every other chrysanthemum I grow. A favorite with most visitors here are the giant anemone-flowered types with their tight boss of petals in the center of the flower or any of the recurves and thistle- or brush-flowered types.

'Salmon Harry Gee' is a British variety that produces gigantic, shaggy-dog blooms if disbudded to a single flower.

CLASSES OF MUMS

All mums, including exhibition and Japanese chrysanthemums, are grouped by class, which helps growers and competitors separate and organize the various types and varieties. Each class requires a unique way of growing and training. Most people are surprised by the many forms they never knew about, such as brush, cascades, bonsai, or anemone-flowered types.

Class 1: Irregular Recurve
We may think of these as "football mums" in the United States, but the Japanese use them almost exclusively in their *kiku* displays. These are also the types of mums used in the *ozukuri* or "thousand bloom" displays so popular at chrysanthemum or *kiku* shows, where hundreds of flowers are achieved from just a single cutting, each one perfectly and precisely arranged on a frame.

Class 2: Reflex
Here the florets each curve downward and the flowers have more of a mop-like effect. The florets are said to overlap, like the feathers on a bird.

Class 3: Regular Incurve
In this flower, each floret curves inward, producing a round-shaped bloom that is more like a ball. These are often very symmetrically arranged.

Class 4: Decorative
A broad term for a mum that is best known as the shape of most hardy garden mums. Shorter florets often curl upwards.

Class 5: Intermediate Incurve
These are similar to both the regular incurve and irregular incurve but are smaller.

Class 6: Pompom
The most popular cutflower mum we know (and hate) from florist shops, but the class also includes some wonderfully exciting forms that are novelties.

Class 7: Single or Semidouble
These are big daisy mums. They're sensationally big if disbudded and pinched.

Class 8: Anemone
These are lovely mums with a tufted center area that looks a lot like a pincushion or a scabiosa.

Class 9: Spoons
Often daisy-like, each floret has an open, tubular end like a spoon.

Class 10: Quill
Similar to the spoon, these also have tubular flower petals but with open ends that are indeed quill-like.

Class 11: Spider
Perhaps the most familiar today, these also produce tubular petals but with great size. Some are so large that they look like fireworks, while others are stiff-petaled and are like starbursts.

Class 12: Brush and Thistle
Odd curiosities, these produce flowerheads not unlike a painter's brush with tubular florets and spikey ends.

Class 13: Unusual
As if brush and thistles weren't curious enough, this class often combines many of the characteristics of other classes. Many of these varieties are very old, from the Edo period, and can be trained in a number of ways, including thousand bloom to traditional *ozukuri* shapes.

WINTER BLOOMS

People are always surprised to hear that winter is my favorite season. I love snowfall, skiing, and the fact that garden chores virtually disappear. I'll admit that having a greenhouse helps a bit too. But even with a conservatory full of plants throughout the winter, inside our home there is no shortage of flowering plants that bring us joy and hopefulness during the long, dark days of winter.

Growing anything green indoors in the winter provides hope, but forcing bulbs into bloom is pure magic. Watching a bowl of paperwhite narcissus or a giant amaryllis bulb come into bloom indoors, with the snow deep outside, is a powerful annual ritual. It also may be the first foray many of us make into the world of gardening.

Indoor winter flowers aren't rare anymore. We can get them almost anywhere, from the supermarket to the garden shop at the hardware store. Maybe it's because these orchids and bromeliads are commercially grown somewhere else then delivered in heated trucks that they feel like a precious commodity. But there is something very satisfying about the authenticity of that small pot of crocuses or that pan of lily of the valley that we've forced into bloom ourselves.

◀ In 1875 Cape Hyacinths, or Lachenalia, were commonly sold as indoor windowsill flowers for chilly, drafty windows. Today they are harder to find, but new breeding is helping. This 'Rupert', a hyrbrid of *L. aloides,* requires no chilling and likes to be planted in well-draining soil. Keep them near a cool and sunny window.

ABOVE: Lily of the Valley pips can be dug from your own garden and forced as well, but they will need a longer chilling period, more like 10 weeks, which can be accomplished in an unheated garage or outdoors in a cold frame. This entire tray of roots and pips were just cut with a spade from our outdoor bed of lily of the valley in early November, chilled under a bench in the greenhouse and then brought indoors under lights to initiate growth where it is warmer.

RIGHT: Read any early 20th-century gardening magazine and you'll see advertisements for Lily of the Valley pips offered for sale to force in the winter. Nearly forgotten by the trade and most home gardeners, the craft is still viable and easy if one just digs their own pips in fall and pots them up, storing them to chill or vernalize as with other bulbs, or one can order pips from the few nurseries who still offer them (see resources page 233).

LEFT: Our garden is in the North Atlantic snow belt in Worcester, Massachusetts, about an hour west of Boston where winter snowfall can be deep for much of the winter thanks to unrelenting nor'easters.

ABOVE: Moving bulbs from the warmth of artificial light back to the greenhouse helps me when certain varieties bloom. This February display on one of the sand beds in the greenhouse shows just how beautiful a winter greenhouse can look. Many of these bulbs come into the house for display in the plant windows.

ABOVE: So common in mild-winter climates, most northern gardeners aren't even aware that the camellia was once the most useful winter-flowering greenhouse flower in the 19th century yet today, few northern florists keep their own greenhouses. The camellia was often featured on Christmas and St. Valentine's Day cards in the Victorian era before flowers could be flown worldwide on jets. In many ways, they were the first 'slow flowers'.

RIGHT: Hybrid crocus are easiest to force, often blooming after just a couple of months in the cold frame. One can also keep them potted in a cold unused refrigerator.

AMARYLLIS

Hippeastrum spp. and hybrids

The amaryllis bulb is about as easy as it gets when it comes to forcing a bulb to bloom. Only the paperwhite narcissus is easier. Problems usually result only from mistreatment of the bulb before it was acquired. Most mail-order nurseries are a safe bet for buying bulbs.

Southern US gardeners may be wondering what all the fuss is about. In Arizona, Texas, and Georgia, forced amaryllis are normally planted directly in the garden after the holiday display. In zones 8 to 11, most amaryllis varieties are hardy enough to survive the mild winter as long as bulbs experience less water for half of their growing season. Botanically there has been disagreement in taxonomy about the genus *Amaryllis*, which to a botanist now refers to a completely different plant. The proper Latin name for our common amaryllis is actually *Hippeastrum*.

Amaryllis bulbs can be expensive, and the price ranges can be extreme. They are graded by size, and you usually get what you pay for. The giant premium bulbs are sold mostly at online dealers or in premium garden centers. A premium bulb as large as a muskmelon can produce up to three flower stalks in a season, and even though they might be three times as expensive, the display can last all winter long. I find these bulbs to be a good investment in the long run.

It's hard to find bad amaryllis bulbs. Look for bulbs that don't have a bud emerging with the stem showing, for often the stem can be damaged by mishandling (dropping the box will do it), resulting in a stem that wants to twist and curl. Look for bulbs with just the bud tip peeking out.

◄ A collection of newer amaryllis hybrids blooming in February on our living room windowsill are not only easy to grow but are fun to watch growing and opening up indoors. We grow these inside all winter because the greenhouse is too cold for them in January and February.

REBLOOMING AMARYLLIS

I rarely encourage home gardeners to try to rebloom their amaryllis, as I believe that it is more work than it is worth. But if you want to try, here are some tips.

- Start with a bulb that bloomed in midwinter and not one specially cultivated to bloom precisely during the holiday season.

- Pot the bulb in good potting mix and water sparingly until the bulb seems well rooted (which can take some time, often after it blooms). Just because it has produced leaves doesn't mean that the bulb has rooted.

- Grow the amaryllis indoors in a bright, sunny window, and move it outside once the weather gets warm in spring. Fertilize with a slow-release, low-nitrogen feed, as the bulb needs to form flower buds before it goes dormant.

- Dry off the bulb and let the foliage go yellow near the end of summer, and move it to a dry, dark spot once the soil is dry.

- Begin watering in late November, or once a flower bud or foliage emerges. Know that it may take 2 years before a flower bud can form again given the stress that the bulb had to endure.

GROWING AN AMARYLLIS

Plant an unrooted amaryllis bulb in a pot just 1 inch (2.5 cm) larger than the bulb itself, as roots will take some time to emerge. Water the soil once and wait until the soil dries out again, as you want to stimulate the bulb to begin growing roots slowly. It's not uncommon for a tall amaryllis in full bloom to tumble out of its container, exposing that it has yet to form roots, and this is when most people fail, as the wet soil has begun to rot the bulb.

Setting bulbs in bulb vases with their bases just touching water or pebbles has become a common way featured on social media and at stylish florists. It may be attractive, but it is not recommended, as the risk of rotting the bulb is even greater.

Amaryllis bulbs in early winter

Amaryllis in pots

Today there are hundreds of varieties of amaryllis to choose from miniatures to giant, late-winter blooming types. With hardly a bad one in the bunch, look more for the quality of the bulb than at the price. Expensive bulbs are often worth the extra cost for they produce more stems with buds, in a sense tripling the display that a bulb with just a single stem would present. One expensive bulb often produces three stems so that a bulb can essentially bloom from January, like this one, until March, which is when this one last bloomed.

TYPES OF AMARYLLIS

Amaryllis bulbs were never a viable commercial crop until the late 1950s. It is believed there are around eight species all native to South America (mostly Brazil and the central Andes in Peru and Bolivia), but populations extend north to Mexico and some Caribbean islands. Some species, like *H. striatum*, have naturalized in mild climates such as Hawaii, where many locals think of them as endemic wildflowers. Modern hybrids have been created using many popular collector species, bringing us all sorts of flower shapes and sizes. Spider-flowered forms with thin petals, often referred to as Cybister types, were developed using the genetics of *H. cybister*, a species with thin, spidery petals that blooms later in the winter. Other types might have miniature blossoms yet produce multiple stems and even variegated foliage. Collectors of pure species are always seeking out the hard-to-find species for their greenhouses or gardens, yet few, if any, do well if grown indoors and are best left to the serious collectors.

If you want to force an amaryllis bulb to bloom for Christmas, be sure to order one described as "Christmas blooming," which means that it has been specially grown and treated to bloom earlier in winter.

'La Paz' is just one of many more exotic forms of Duth Amaryllis being offered to home growers. It looks more horticultural than the broad-petaled hybrids but is just as easy to grow for mid-winter color on a windowsill.

A collection of amaryllis usually looks better than just one, especially when displayed together as their colors enhance each other. With a blizzard blowing beyond the window, what could be better to warm a gardener's heart?

Amaryllis 'Exotic Star' shows how modern plant breeding is broadening what we all think of as an amaryllis. It looks more like an orchid with its veined petals and large flowers.

PAPERWHITES

Narcissus papyraceus

Writing about how to grow paperwhites in a gardening book is sort of like including a recipe for peanut butter and jelly sandwiches in a cookbook. Paperwhites are the gateway plant for many future gardeners, for nothing could be easier. Pebbles plus water equals blooms in just a few weeks.

Paperwhites are Mediterranean *narcissi*, native from Morocco through Spain to Turkey. Today we associate the paperwhite with the holiday season. The name "paperwhite" comes from the Egyptian papyrus, as it produced the whitest paper in biblical times. There's no need to go into detail about growing this bulb for blooms, as they will come to flower either in pure water and pebbles or in a bulb vase with just water. Paperwhites will naturalize in mild climates, yet for the most part, you still need to force them indoors for holiday blooms. Forcing may not be the right term, however, for there are a handful of narcissus species that all come into bloom not after a cold winter, but after a dry season of rest.

Most of the bulbs we find today are commercially grown in Israel, North Africa, or India and come to us via the Dutch bulb markets. Opinions about their scent are polarized, as some love it and others can only smell cat pee. I adore it and can't have enough, but know that breeders are well aware of these opinions and have been able to breed sweet-smelling varieties as well as some that have little scent at all.

◀ Even though paperwhite narcissus should be grown in pebbles and water, they can grow well if planted in potting soil (be sure the pot has a drainage hole).

Timing paperwhite blubs for Christmas or New Year's depends on the temperature of your growing medium, but generally, speaking bulbs will bloom 4 or 5 weeks after planting. Thanksgiving weekend is my traditional time to plant paperwhites at home to get Christmas flowers. Pebbles, marbles, or small stones in a container that doesn't leak is all that is needed. Bury the bulbs halfway up their necks. A cold windowsill will slow down their growth, so find a warm, bright spot to keep them growing quickly.

I prefer to pot my paperwhite bulbs just as I would any Dutch bulb being forced: with potting soil and a topdressing of sheet moss or pebbles to hold them in. I like the look better, and the bulbs grow stronger and are rooted into the soil better. The pots must have drainage though, which works well as I have a greenhouse, but I'll admit that this method may not work for everyone.

Tip

You can reduce the height of paperwhites being forced in water and pebbles by adding a bit of alcohol to the water. Often called "pickling," alcohol will shorten their height by at least one-third. Add ¼ cup (60 ml) of vodka, gin, or any clear spirit to 4 cups (1 L) of water and replace the water after the first week.

CHRISTMAS CACTUS

Schlumbergera spp.

Great confusion exists about holiday cactus. It might help to know that the common Christmas cactus, *Schlumbergera*, are tropical rain forest plants and not desert plants. As such, they appreciate warm, humid environments and plenty of water while growing in a quick-draining organic medium. Their needs are exactly opposite of cactus-like.

Most Christmas cactus today are hybrids or interspecific crosses. Botanically they are known as *S. truncata* hybrids, and their common name could be either Thanksgiving cactus or Christmas cactus, depending on when that particular variety blooms. Generally they all naturally bloom between October and December in the Northern Hemisphere. You may see the name *Zygocactus* used on Christmas cactus plant tags, but that is incorrect. The later-blooming species are neither *Zygocactus* or *Schlumbergera*, they are *Rhipsalidopsis*, a closely related genus, that requires similar care.

GROWING CHRISTMAS CACTUS

Use a good-quality potting mix with plenty of organic matter. Christmas cactus often suffer from yellowing leaves and slow growth. If your plants are turning chlorotic or pale rather than bright green, be sure that they are not exposed to full sunlight in the summer, and then repot them. The reason is most likely that the plant's roots cannot access iron and manganese from the soil, something that naturally happens once the soil pH drops below 5.5.

You don't need to get your pH meter, however. Just go ahead and repot your plant into a good-quality professional potting mix. This will ensure that the pH has already been adjusted for you. *Schlumbergera* are very sensitive to even slight pH shifts, and commercial growers are advised to monitor their pH every few weeks to keep it precisely at 5.5 so plants stay beautiful and green. All the nitrogen in the world or fish emulsion won't do a thing; it's more about electrical conductivity and pH.

Christmas cactus like to grow without stress, which includes moderately warm temperatures (70°F to 75°F [21°C to 24°C]) and constant watering. Adding fresh soil if they need it will boost their growth. A slow-release, balanced plant food is helpful to keep them from going hungry. In early spring, snap off the tips on all branches, and you will double your flowers next year. To get plants blooming on schedule, expose them only to natural day length, especially in late summer and autumn. Keep Christmas cactus plants in a room that has windows but no lights on at night, and move plants there after keeping them outdoors away from street lights until frost threatens and until flower buds form.

◀ Today, Christmas cactus come in a wide range of colors and forms. Look for heirloom varieties and rare mutations like the variegated 'Madame Butterfly' that are sometimes shared by collectors at cactus and succulent society auctions.

TENDER INDOOR BULBS

In addition to paperwhites and amaryllis, there are many bulbs you can grow indoors that bloom with little care other than tending to their natural growth cycles. Most come from deep in the Southern Hemisphere. While some are from South America, particularly the Andes, most come from South Africa, where winter weather is wet and summer is dry. Often referred to as "Cape bulbs," most gardeners are familiar with some of them, such as freesia and calla lily, but less so with the others.

The Cape bulbs have always been popular with greenhouse growers, as most are winter-blooming plants. But as heated homes made their culture more difficult in the mid-20th century, many disappeared from grower lists. Any gardening book from before 1900 may list hundreds of Cape bulbs, however, as they were perfectly designed for long ocean travel on sailing ships, and it was often these same merchants who could afford to keep heated greenhouses in the north and service horticultural societies of the time.

Veltheimia bracteata 'Yellow Flame' is a rare yellow form of this easy winter-blooming houseplant.

◄ Order tender indoor bulbs in August and pot-up by September in well-draining potting soil. Water once and set in a bright, cool place (even outdoors until frost threatens) until growth begins. Then bring into greenhouse or set in a cool, sunny plant window to eventually come into bloom in early winter.

There are many winter-blooming tender bulbs that were once common windowsill plants a hundred years ago. *Veltheimia bracteata* is one of them, but this rare selection is more uncommon with its pink and cream blossoms. Specialty bulb catalogs often feature more unusual color selections, but even the common pink form is lovely, and makes a long-lived houseplant.

Lachenalia viridiflora is often the first of the Cape Hyacinths to bloom in the greenhouse. Pots are brought indoors for display in the plant windows until Christmas, but one could try growing these in a cool sunroom or chilly bedroom window as the bulbs don't need pre-chilling, just a dry, warm summer's rest without water. That said, bulbs will be difficult to find.

Indoors, a few of the Cape bulbs can be grown in a sunny, cool plant window or in an unheated room, perhaps. Many plants in the hyacinth family (such as the veltheimia) grow well this way, and some in the amaryllis family, like cyrtanthus or fire lilies, have long been considered excellent Victorian houseplants. The secret is to find the coolest and brightest place for them to grow.

Veltheimia bracteata was considered a common house-plant in the early 20th century. It grows well in even warmer temperatures, so it is an excellent starter plant for this journey. Look for them listed in Dutch bulb catalogs or from specialty bulb growers. They are mainly pink selections, but rarer yellow and near-white varieties are worth looking for and are often sought by collectors. The bulbs don't require anything fancy, just general potting mix and a bit of fertilizer lower in nitrogen once or twice a winter.

Plants will go dormant by spring and should be kept dry until fall, when watering should commence. Bulbs divide easily, and these offsets can be potted up while dormant and shared with friends.

Lachenalia, a genus also related to hyacinths, had their day in the mid-19th century when almost every cold green-house kept pots of them for winter blooms. This South African plant often goes by the name Cape Hyacinth, and while dozens of species exist, a few are beginning to make a comeback among bulb collectors. A new strain named African Beauty® is being marketed for commercial growers as a pot plant, and sometimes pots are seen at nurseries being sold as an Easter plant. Often no one buys them as they are not familiar with them.

Most *Lachenalia* require the same growing conditions. Bulbs, which are easy to find online if you are looking for

Of all the rare teal-colored bulbs, some a very rare like this *Lachenalia aloides* subsp. Vanzyliae justify making cool winter greenhouses popular again as they once were in the mid-19th century.

The African Beauty® series of *Lachenalia* or Cape Hyacinths don't require prechilling and are as easy to grow as paperwhites, yet they have been challenging to introduce to growers simply because people are not familiar with them.

the new African Beauty® series in various colors, are potted up in the late summer or early fall. They are as foolproof as a paperwhite narcissus if grown in a sunny, cold window or greenhouse. You may be able to find the non-hybrid species forms, which were tremendously popular 200 years ago but not so much today.

The easiest indoor bulbs to cultivate, and the most lovely, are *L. aloides* and its many subspecies like quadricolor. It's called *aloides* because the flowers look like that of an aloe. The rarer *L. viridiflora* has incredible teal-blue flowers that often bloom earlier, at Christmastime. Allowed to dry out in spring and kept dry all summer still in their pot, these should all emerge again once watering commences in mid-September, often just as cooler weather begins to arrive, which naturally will trigger their growth.

If you have a greenhouse that doesn't freeze, all *Lachenalia* are good performers in the winter, and all are easy to grow from seed. You can often purchase from specialty seed companies in South Africa or from Rock Garden Society seed exchanges. Sown 3 inches (7 cm) deep in pots in the autumn, the seedlings often bloom within 3 years. This is often the most cost-effective way to get any Cape bulb.

Tecophilaea cyanocrocus is on the fringe of being growable indoors, but as a blue-flowered gem, its bulbs are sometimes worth the one-shot deal to get them to bloom indoors. Getting a rebloom the following year might be challenging without a greenhouse, but who cares? Find a spot that is 55°F (13°C) in the winter.

CAMELLIA

Camellia sinensis

Cultivated for centuries in China and Japan, the camellia is a common winter flowering shrub in zones 10 and higher. This includes much of the Deep South in the United States, most of the northern Pacific Coast, and many mild-winter areas in Europe and Australia. With over 3,000 hybrids and over 200 species, the camellia has surely captured the hearts of many during its hundreds of years in cultivation. Today, outside of where they grow outdoors, they have virtually disappeared, and most northern gardeners have never even seen a live camellia blossom unless they have traveled.

This wasn't always the case. Throughout much of the 18th and 19th centuries, the camellia reigned as the primary winter flower grown in cold greenhouses in the north, where glass greenhouses and pit houses were once commonplace. Camellias where also grown commercially outside of the large cities and delivered by train or carriage for winter use.

As a houseplant, camellias cannot live in our modern dry-heated and climate-controlled homes. But camellias are discovering a new fan base anyway, as their beauty is driving many to consider building an indoor winter garden in an unheated breezeway, where many cool-growing winter pit-house plants like citrus and jasmine can be grown. What camellias hate are hot, dry temperatures in which buds that were set the previous summer outdoors will drop instantly.

◂ 'Lipstick' is a newer anemone-form camellia that grow well in a small pot and produces copious amounts of this uniquely formed flower.

The rose form in camellia is often favored by growers because its petals are arranged in a symetrical pattern. 'Nuccio's Gem' is a popular variety and blooms every January in our greenhouse.

Difficult to grow indoors, one can keep camellia shrubs in large pots on an unheated porch that remains above freezing, or in that 'special' place where winter temperatures stay in the 40s and bright sunlight is available such as a mud room with windows or a bright garage where natural light streams in.

Camellias prefer to be potbound, so the pots you grow them in don't need to be large. While camellias are a bit challenging to find, a few online sources exist (see Resources, page 233). Potted plants need little care if grown outdoors in the summer. Greenhouse plants are typically brought outdoors in early April in the north, as occasional light freezes do little damage unless the plants have tender new growth. In the autumn, plants can stay outside until temperatures dip below 20°F (-7°C), when the roots or flower buds can be damaged.

Fertility needs for indoor bulbs are easy to meet. Basic topdressing of new soil applied each spring is all that is needed. Camellias like a high-acid soil mix, usually one with peat or acidic composted bark. Nurseries use cotton-seed meal as a nitrogen source, which can be applied to the surface of the soil once a year in spring.

Camellias can be organized into three groups or types, plus many species. The sasanqua camellias are the first to bloom in the autumn, just as the leaves begin to turn. *Camellia japonica* is the largest group with the most hybrids

'Kaleidoscope' is a 2019 introduction from Nuccio's Nurseries that grows upright and produces sweet, single pale pink and striped flowers in February.

Camellia 'Brushfield's Yellow' produces a pale, yellow blossom on a nicely branched plant.

(over 2,000), and they have what most feel are the prettiest and most classic-looking flowers. *C. reticulata* types and their many hybrids are also pretty. Then there are countless crosses between species and many floral types ranging from the large single or Higo camellias with a boss of yellow stamens in the middle, all the way to nearly yellow or fragrant camellias. Anemone-flowered types have a crested center of a flower, and many have multicolored flowers (red-and-white peppermint striped) and even variegated foliage.

Peak season for camellias is around Valentine's Day, and since their color palette is primarily pink, red, and white, there is a market for northern flower farmers with unheated hoop houses to rediscover the merits of the camellia. By mid-February, the greenhouse is so full of camellias (some of which are planted directly into the ground) that I can bring bowls and plates of their colorful flowers into the house on most days. Displaying in plates or bowls is traditional, as they have very short woody stems, so carefully snip off flowers one by one.

CLIVIA
Clivia spp.

As the South African-native clivia becomes more accessible, many home gardeners are discovering their striking blooms and luxurious green or variegated strap-shaped leaves. Outdoors in California or in warm, Mediterranean climates, where they are often used as a groundcover perennial, the clivia is as resilient as a cactus and can handle long periods of drought.

As houseplants, clivias have long been considered to be rare and expensive connoisseur plants. The standard orange-flowered *Clivia miniata* is the most common, but many novelty forms and color variations have always been horticultural currency among serious collectors. Some of the highest prices ever spent on a plant have been on yellow clivia. Today, many other mutations and forms have become more accessible. Prices have dropped for common forms but have risen for the one-of-a-kind specimens.

Clivia cyrtanthiflora group seedling forms beautifully large plants with pendant blossoms every winter.

◀ We've been collecting clivia for decades, even traveling to Japan to acquire rare plants. Our own breeding, casual as it is, still produces beautiful variations in color, form, and foliage. It's hard to choose which ones to keep and which ones to give away to friends.

One of our Clivia interspecific crosses (*Cyrtanthiflora* group) that blooms for us every January. We aren't the sort to register it, so we named it after a dear lost pet 'Muggle Drops.'

Commercially, what brings the price of a new plant down is micropropagation: isolating cells that can grow into clones quickly. The clivia is one of those rare plants that remains stubborn about being micropropagated. Few, if any, true clones exist, and while named strains are more common, they come with variability and diversity. This keeps named varieties very rare. They must be divisions of the mother plant as seedlings will vary. Seedlings, especially those raised at home, are easy and fun to grow, and this diversity and variability suddenly becomes a good thing.

What gets a clivia to bloom isn't withholding water or keeping them rootbound, which are both common myths shared on social media. Clivias are very much like Christmas cactus, as their blooming is tied to day length and temperature shifts at night. Like many plants, clivia is stimulated by seasonal changes in its environment. The length of complete darkness at nights and a drop in night-time temperatures tell them that it is time to bloom, as spring is surely coming. If they are being grown in a living room or where there are lamps nearby in the winter, their schedule will be thrown off.

The clivia flowers should have already been formed a year in advance deep inside their thick stalks (clivia are actually geophytes and behave very much like bulbs). If you don't believe me, think about the onion, which is a true bulb. It has modified leaf scales that form the bulb, and a flower bud is dormant deep inside, waiting for spring. Also consider the leek, botanically also an allium, but one that doesn't go completely dormant. A clivia is like a leek in this sense.

Starting clivia from seed is easy and fun. Their large fruit will turn color (red for orange varieties and yellow for yellow ones). When the pods are soft, crush them carefully in your hand and remove the half dozen or so big seeds that look remarkably like macadamia nuts. Sow these in fresh potting mix, covering them with ¼ to ½ inch (6 to 13 mm) of soil, and water lightly until you see leaves. Clivias grow slowly, one to four leaves a year, so don't expect seedlings to bloom until 4 to 6 years after planting. Still, they look good almost instantly with their single strap-like leaves and thick, fleshy roots.

As a houseplant, a clivia is nearly indestructible. Water when dry, repot every few years just to keep the soil fresh, and keep your plant in a cool room that experiences mostly natural light for the winter if you want it to bloom in February or March. Fall-blooming clivias seem to have fewer problems blooming if they spend their summers outside under trees.

CLIVIA FACTS

Clivia is pronounced "klye-vee-ah," as they were named in honor of Lady Charlotte Florentia Clive when the plant was first collected in South Africa the early 1800s. It turns out that clivia reacts to the photoperiod, like so many other plants. Day length (actually, it's the night length) is vital, along with temperature shifts that signal to the plant that spring or fall has arrived. Forget old advice about being potbound or withholding water. Getting a clivia to bloom is simply exposure to seasonal day-length shifts and cooler night temperatures. Today, there are six species of clivia in the genus and many interspecific crosses, which are relatively new on the scene since clivia breeding is only about 25 years old. The standard orange *C. miniata* has been bred by breeders and is available in countless shades of reddish-orange, near pinkish-orange, and pure yellow. Some rarer ones some fetch thousands of dollars.

Today there are plenty of yellow selections, and while a few are still costly, a couple have been micropropagated *invitro* (something that has eluded most clivia), keeping their cost high for special varieties or color forms. Some good clivia strains still sell for well over $1,000 each. Most clivia today are seed raised, and a yellow plant crossed with a yellow or even itself will produce mostly yellow offspring, each slightly different from its parent.

FORCED HARDY FLOWERS

Forcing bulbs is perhaps the oldest horticultural craft that is still practiced. Bulbs are magical in that they have preformed flower buds deep inside their bulb already and are just waiting for spring weather to arrive after a long winter. The premise is simple, really. We pot bulbs up while they are dormant, provide them with cold temperatures just above freezing for some time (around 12 to 16 weeks at 38°F to 40°F [3°C to 4°C]) and then gradually bring their pots into a fake spring indoors, where they bloom and comfort us during the depths of winter.

The easiest Dutch flower bulbs to force are hyacinths, narcissus (daffodils), and crocus, but many of the so-called lesser bulbs like the species crocus, scillas, and *Iris reticulata* are almost easier, if not faster, to bring into bloom.

Forcing bulbs was common practice in the 19th century, when special glassforcing vases were designed by glass blowers. In these vessels, a chilled bulb (usually a hyacinth) could sit on the top. Many bulb-forcing pieces of specialty pottery were also designed, but few exist today. Florists, estate gardeners, and greenhouses traditionally potted up many bulbs in clay pots to provide winter color for homes, gifts, and floral work. Brought into a cool greenhouse or onto a cold windowsill, pots could be gradually warmed up after their

Iris reticulata force quickly and are one of the easiest for beginners. Sometimes we can have them blooming just a few weeks after New Year's.

allotted time period and eventually brought into the home or conservatory to complete their display. With the advent of the big spring flower shows, many cities featured elaborate bulb displays in midwinter that warmed people's hearts and suggested that spring was just around the corner.

◄ Our plant window in the dining room is full of fragrant, flowering spring plants starting in late January and lasting with frequent rotations until mid-March.

Most anyone today can force bulbs, even without a greenhouse or even a cold frame. All that is needed is to pot bulbs early enough (usually mid-October for January and February forcing). Hyacinths, most narcissus (particularly the dwarf varieties), and early tulips such as the Darwins do well. *I. reticulata*, all the muscari (grape hyacinths), and the smaller species crocus are even easier to bring into bloom, as they force quickly in January, just when you really need some color and fragrance.

Pot your bulbs tightly, shoulder to shoulder—touching is okay, even encouraged, as many bulbs like to be tight next to each other, particularly narcissus. Bulbs generally like company. Plastic pots are best, and you can use any soil mix that can hold moisture. Nutrients aren't as important as water retention. A good commercial potting mix will do. I apply a topdressing of gravel as well, which not only looks good but helps keep the soil in place when watering.

The greatest challenge you'll face when forcing winter bulbs is how to properly chill the bulbs. Some people use an old refrigerator, which works fine. Even an extra beer cooler set onto an unheated porch can hold a few pots of potted bulbs.

The trick is to keep the bulbs dark and cold, just above freezing at all times, until the proper time to force them. In milder climates, you might be able to bury pots in a big plastic garbage bag full of dried leaves and leave it outside. Others have a secret cold spot, such as in a cellar stairwell or a garage. One old method still practiced in rural areas is to dig a pit 3 feet (1 m) deep and fill it with sand and then dried leaves in which to bury the pots.

After 12 to 16 weeks, bring in the pots, especially those with the bulb noses or shoots already emerging. The quickest to bloom will be the species crocus and the *I. reticulata* pots, followed by narcissus and hyacinths, and lastly the tulips, which often are the most challenging to please.

Our plant window in the dining room is full of fragrant, flowering spring plants starting in February.

Forcing bulbs can be planted close together, shoulder-to-shoulder.

Bulbs need to chill for 12 or more weeks below 38° F. but not freezing.

Gradually introduce bulbs to warmer temperatures once they show signs of growth.

Tulips often need darkness with warmth at first to help extend their stems.

Iris reticulat and cocus are some of the easiest to force.

Displays of forced bulbs and other winter blooming plants on window-sills helps us survive long winters indoors.

FORCED
LILY OF THE VALLEY

Convallaria majalis

Gardening magazines in the early to mid–20th century used to feature ads for lily of the valley "pips" for winter forcing. They were long grown by northern nurseries and flower farms in the 18th and 19th centuries, as glass and steam heat became more popular. The idea of forcing plants like scented Parma violets became popular near big cities, where winters the joy of fresh flowers meant profitable crops for farmers and nurseries. The lily of the valley found a niche and quickly became popular as a winter-forced cut flower in Europe and in North America.

Weddings around the turn of the 20th century demanded so many lily of the valley that ice houses would store dormant pips for florists to force throughout the entire year. French farmers had elaborate methods for growing what they called *muguet*, and lily of the valley is still grown in southern France for the perfume industry. A bit of a runner outdoors in the garden, many old gardens in the north have areas that are carpeted with mats of lily of the valley. What few people know, however, is that you can still dig a section of these clumps and force the pips for winter bloom indoors just as it was done 150 years ago.

Pips can also be ordered from France or Belgium via the few bulb importers who still carry them, but the days of forcing lily of the valley seemed to have vanished. These specially grown pips, which are still cultivated for the cutflower industry, are a bit larger, but garden-grown plants produce flowers that are nearly as large.

Dig lily of the valley up from the garden once the foliage has faded in late October or early November. You can choose to wash the roots to isolate each crown (or pip). Choose those with blunt shoots, as they produce the flower stalks. Or you can just use a spade to cut out a section from the bed. Set the cuttings in a plastic seedling flat with drainage holes, as you will need to set this somewhere for the first half of the winter. The lily of the valley will need chilling for at least 10 weeks, just like any forced bulb, except these can periodically handle light freezing.

Washed pips can be replanted close together in potting soil in a pot with drainage and then stored somewhere cold. Near freezing is best, but ideally somewhere between 25°F and 38°F (–4°C and 3°C). A porch, under a porch, or in a cooler set outside is good, as the pips will maintain a constant cold temperature if they are set in the shade.

Forced lily of the valley requires warm temperatures in which to grow—70°F to 75°F (21°C to 24°C) is ideal. The earlier you start them, the longer they will take to come into bloom. Christmas and New Year's flowers are probably unrealistic, but you should have flowers for Valentine's Day or even later. Move pots to a sunny window once the flower buds appear and enjoy the fragrance.

◄ Lily of the Valley pips can by ordered online and potted up in December for forcing in winter, or you can dig up pads of your own pips from the garden in early November, and if kept cold (not freezing) until mid-January, force your own indoors.

RESOURCES

LILY OF THE VALLEY PIPS

White Flower Farm
www.whiteflowerfarm.com
White Flower Farm frequently offers imported lily of the valley pips for forcing (order in late autumn for December delivery) as well as some of the largest sized and newest amaryllis varieties available in North America. An exclusive source for pretrained 'tree' wisteria plants.

HARDY AND TENDER FORCING BULBS

Old House Gardens
www.oldhousegardens.com
North America's premier source for heirloom bulbs including antique 'broken' tulips, double hyacinths, gladiolus, heirloom dahlias, and more.

McClure & Zimmerman
www.mzbulb.com
Excellent commercial source for both tender and hardy Dutch imported bulbs. They publish a spring and autumn catalog. Often carry some limited varieties of rarities like Tecophilia, Lachenalia, and Velthiemia.

Brent and Becky's Bulbs
www.brentandbeckysbulbs.com
Full selections of Dutch and American-grown bulbs, particularly narcissus but also prechilled bulbs for forcing, and for southern gardeners. They also carry indoor bulbs, Christmas Amaryllis, and a good selection of paperwhite narcissus varieties.

John Scheepers
www.johnscheepers.com
Well-known American importer of fine Dutch bulbs, both tender and hardy.

Van Engelen Inc.
www.vanengelen.com
The wholesale site for John Scheepers offering discounts on larger quantities of imported Dutch bulbs.

Telos Rare Bulbs
www.telosrarebulbs.com
Some of the hardest-to-find rare bulbs all grown in their northern California nursery. Extraordinary collection of many greenhouse and tender bulbs like Lachenalia, Oxalis, Tecophilea and more.

Odyssey Bulbs
www.odysseybulbs.com
Good specialty and rare-bulb catalog for very unusual hardy bulbs especially crocus, fritillaria and colchicum.

Rareplants
(formerly Paul Christian Rare Bulbs)
www.rareplants.co.uk
An ever-changing seasonal collection of rare and collector bulbs, both tender and hardy—some very rare. Ships most bulbs to US and Canada, others require CITES certificate.

IRIS

Schreiner's Iris Gardens
www.schreinersgardens.com
A large family-run 100 acre Bearded iris farm with many of their own introductions and award-winning iris not typically found in the trade.

Joe Pye Weed's Garden
www.jpwflowers.com
A small specialty nursery long dediated to breeding and introducing Siberian irises, Versicolor iris and Interspecific hybrids. Only ships to US and Canada.

Aitken's Salmon Creek Garden
https://flowerfantasy.net
Comprehensive selection of bearded, border and Siberian irises.

GLADIOLUS

Honker Flats
www.honkerflats.com
Nice selection of newer crosses of gladilous as well as other plants.

Pleasant Valley Glads and Dahlias
www.gladiola.com
Big selection of farm-raised gladiolus and dahlias.

PEONIES

Song Sparrow Gardens
www.songsparrow.com

Peony's Envy
https://www.peonysenvy.com

Hollingsworth Peonies
https://www.hollingsworthpeonies.com

Cricket Hill Garden
www.treepeony.com

RARE PERENNIALS AND OTHER FLOWERING PLANTS

Plant Delights
www.plantdelights.com

Digging Dog
https://www.diggingdog.com
Rare perennials and other plants

Far Reaches Farms
https://www.farreachesfarm.com/Default.asp

Kartuz Greenhouses
www.kartuz.com

Blackmore & Langdon
www.blackmore-langdon.com
British source for world-class delphiniums and tuberous begonias.

ANNUAL SEED

Baker Creek Heirloom Seeds
www.rareseeds.com

Swallowtailgardens.com
http://swallowtailgardenseeds.com

Fedco Seeds
www.fedcoseeds.com

Territorial Seed
http://www.territorialseed.com

Adaptive Seeds
https://www.adaptiveseeds.com

Silverhill Seeds
www.silverhillseeds.co.za
South African seed source for a massive collection of wild-collected seeds shipped worldwide—many unusual annual flowers native to South Africa like Ceretotheca and Lachenalia seed.

Jelitto Seeds
www.jelitto.com
Imported seeds for many annuals, biennials and perennials. Prechilled and pretreated seed as well especially for primroses, delphinium, and holyhocks.

ANNUAL PLANTS

Annies Annuals
www.anniesannuals.com

SPENCER SWEET PEA SEED

Enchanting Sweet Peas
www.enchantingsweetpeas.com

Renee's Garden
www.reneesgarden.com

SWEET PEAS AND OTHER FLOWER SEEDS

Floret Flowers
https://shop.floretflowers.com
Cut flower seeds, dahlia tubers, and bulbs

Siskiyouseeds
www.siskiyouseeds.com

Owl's Acre
www.owlsacreseeds.co.uk

Roger Parsons Sweet Peas
www.rpsweetpeas.com
Excellent selection of all sweet peas including Spencer varieties, novelties, and species.

SEEDS—SPECIALTY ANNUALS

Larner Seeds
www.larnerseeds.com
An extensive list of native Californian annuals and other wildflowers for naturalizing or for gardens. Good source for fresh seed of cool-growing Californian natives often available in bulk quantities including clarkia, gilia, layia, Limnanthes, nemophila, phacelia, and more.

Eden Brothers
www.edenbrothers.com
Huge collection of flower seeds (more than 40 varieties of annual poppies alone).

Silver Falls Seed Company

www.silverfallsseed.com
Specializing in North American natives and western wildflowers including hard-to-find mallows, clarkias, and phacelias to name a few.

Chiltern Seeds (UK)

www.chilternseeds.co.uk
A comprehensive selection of interesting, rare and hybrid garden seeds including many choice annuals.

Johnny's Selected Seeds

www.johnnyseeds.com
Excellent source for many seeds for both professional farmers and home gardeners.

Select Seeds

www.selectseeds.com
Fine selection of hard-to-find and common flowering annuals and vegetables.

PRIMROSES

Barnhaven Primroses

www.barnhaven.com
Plestin-les-Grèves, France
Barnhaven name is synonymous with the 'worlds finest primroses,' particularly polyanthus types. Mail order currently available to much of Europe, and seed (sometimes plants but subject to government regulations) to North America.

Pops Plants

www.popsplants2.co.uk
Finest award-wining auriculas, alpine auricula, show auricula and edges, selfs and fancies. Often can ship dormant and clean plants without soil to North America subject to USDA regulations.

Wrightman Alpines

https://www.wrightmanalpines.com
Specialty alpine nursery in New Brunswick, Canada

Sequim Rare Plants

http://sequimrareplants.com
Fine, small nursery in Washington State with many rare plants including primroses.

CHRYSANTHEMUMS

Kings Mums, US

www.kingsmums.com
North America's only nursery dedicated to chrysanthemums. Fine source for a full selection of cuttings for both cut flower, Japanese and exhibition mums.

Capobianco Creations

www.capocreations2wixsite.com
John Capobianco is an independent chrysanthemum enthusiast and pro-grower who offers a limited selection of cuttings to US growers. Often has fancy European and hard-to-find English varieties.

Ivor Mace

www.Ivormace.com (UK only)
Independent Chrysanthemum enthusiast and mum-evangelist. The UK's top grower of show mums, sells cuttings and very active on social media, particularly Facebook and YouTube, providing updates and growing tips.

Woolmans

www.woolmans.com
Chrysanthemum cuttings (shipping only to UK and parts of the EU)

DAHLIAS

Dahlia Addict

Dahliaaddict.com
Not a nursery, but a database where you can search for a particular variety and suppliers are suggested throughout North America.

Connell's Dahlias

https://connells-dahlias.com

Dahlia Barn

https://www.dahliabarn.com

Lobaugh's Dahlias

https://lobaughsdahlias.com/product-category/dahlia/

Stone House Dahlias

https://stonehousedahlias.com/shop/
Online seller of rooted dahlia cuttings.

Swan Island Dahlias

www.dahlias.com

INDEX

ACKNOWLEDGMENTS

Many thanks to those who helped by opening their gardens and sharing or finding plants for me (often at the last minute). Thanks go to Michele and Robert Hanss (lilacs and peonies), Darrell Probst (coreopsis), Helen O'Donnell and Bunker Farm (for sharing poppy seedlings), Grace Lam and Five Forks Farms (those Dahlias!), Judith Sellers, Susan Schnare, Amy Olmsted (potted Primroses), Kate Wollensac Freeborn (lilacs) and to Brian at Kings Mums for rooting me cuttings (even though they were officially sold out). I am more than grateful for the team at Cool Spring Press and Quarto Publishing, particularly recognizing the skills and talents of my editors Thom O'hearn, Mark Johanson, and Nyle Vialet for knowing when to push me (or when to pull me back), and to the Art Director, Heather Godin, for the patience and having to entertain an author who happens to also be a graphic designer with strong, often irrational opinions. Last, but not least, to Joseph Philip for tolerating take-out dinners, last minute photoshoots and endless excuses about book deadlines.

MEET MATT MATTUS

Matt Mattus is a life-long gardener, still caring for a two-acre garden that family built in 1906 located in an unassuming city neighborhood in Worcester, Massachusetts. Along with his life partner Joe Philip grow most of the flowers and plants found in this book. Their gardens and glass greenhouse are well known amongst plant enthusiasts. Author of the book 'Mastering the Art of Vegetable Gardening' Matt also writes the popular gardening blog Growingwithplants.com. Known for his in-depth gardening projects and home-trials, readers may recognize his work from features in magazines like Martha Stewart Living or Better Homes and Gardens. Matt has earned a reputation as a not only as a knowledgeable plantsman but is considered an authority on many horticultural subjects ranging from South African Bulbs, to alpine plants and long-forgotten 19th century horticultural practices.

His lectures are popular at botanic gardens around the country where he speaks on these and other gardening topics sharing stunning photos and inspiring audiences with interesting plants – often documenting his latest botanizing trip to an exotic local such as the Himalaya or western China. Matt currently sits on the board of Tower Hill Botanic Garden, serves as Vice President and Trustee of the 175-year-old Worcester County Horticultural Society, and is past president of the North American Rock Garden Society (NARGS). He is also very active in many specialist plant societies.